gideon

PRISCILLA SHIRER

Lifeway Press® • Brentwood, Tennessee

© 2022 Priscilla Shirer

No part of this book may be reproduced or transmitted in any form or by any means, electronic or mechanical, including photocopying and recording, or by any information storage or retrieval system, except as may be expressly permitted in writing by the publisher. Requests for permission should be addressed in writing to Lifeway Press; 200 Powell Place, Suite 100; Brentwood, TN 37027-7707.

ISBN 978-1-0877-8909-5
Item 005843057

Dewey decimal classification: 222.32
Subject headings: GIDEON \ BIBLE. O.T. JUDGES 6-8 \ CHRISTIAN LIFE

Unless otherwise noted, Scripture quotations are taken from the New American Standard Bible®, copyright © 1960, 1962, 1963, 1968, 1971, 1972, 1973, 1975, 1977, 1995 by the Lockman Foundation. Used by permission.
Scripture quotations identified HCSB are from the Holman Christian Standard Bible, copyright © 1999, 2000, 2002, 2003, 2009 by Holman Bible Publishers. Used by permission. Holman Christian Standard Bible® and HCSB® are federally registered trademarks of Holman Bible Publishers.
Scripture quotations identified NIV are from the New International Version, copyright © 1973, 1978, 1984 by International Bible Society.
Scripture quotations identified NKJV are from the New King James Version. Copyright © 1979, 1980, 1982, Thomas Nelson Inc. Publishers. Used by permission.
Scripture quotations marked NLT are taken from the Holy Bible, New Living Translation, copyright © 1996. Used by permission of Tyndale House Publishers, Inc., Wheaton, IL 60189 USA. All rights reserved.

To order additional copies of this resource, write to Lifeway Resources Customer Service; 200 Powell Place, Suite 100; Brentwood, TN 37027-7707; fax 615.251.5933; phone toll free 800.458.2772; email orderentry@lifeway.com; or order online at www.lifeway.com.

Printed in the United States of America

Adult Ministry Publishing
Lifeway Resources
200 Powell Place, Suite 100
Brentwood, TN 37027-7707

TABLE OF CONTENTS

PRISCILLA SHIRER is a wife and mom first, but put a Bible in her hand and a message in her heart, and you'll see why thousands meet God in powerful, personal ways at her conferences.

With a master's degree in biblical studies from Dallas Theological Seminary, Priscilla brings the depths of Scripture to life. Her nine Bible studies span such topics as the Exodus, hearing the voice of God, and biblical characters like Jonah and Gideon. She has also written seven books, including the *New York Times* bestseller *The Resolution for Women*.

She and her husband, Jerry, lead Going Beyond Ministries, through which they provide spiritual training, support, and resources to the body of Christ. They count it as their greatest privilege to serve every denomination and culture across the spectrum of the church.

Between writing and studying, you'll probably find her at home cleaning up after (and trying to satisfy the appetites of) her three rapidly growing boys.

www.GoingBeyond.com

INTRODUCTION

Hey there, my friend, I've been waiting for you. Really, I have.

I've looked forward with great anticipation and much prayer to sharing these weeks of Bible study with you. For two years now, my dining room table has been crowded with Bibles, commentaries, study notes, aged articles—all to help discover what God might teach us through one of Scripture's most intriguing characters. My family has heard me talk about this epic story so much, they're starting to get that glazed look in their eyes as soon as I mention Gideon. They might know more about him now than I do. So they'll be relieved to know that his name and story are now in your hands ... and off the dining room table.

Dinner anyone?

While we're talking about food, I hope you came hungry—starving even. I pray that every time you watch the sessions or sit down for your personal devotions in this workbook, you will voraciously seek a fresh touch from God. We should never approach God's Word *with a casualness or indifference* ... even when we're looking at one character in three little chapters of the Bible.

So if you're feeling a little empty right now, don't despair. Hunger only devastates when we have nothing to satisfy it. But in these pages, you will find a table divinely set for you. We're about to feast on a lavish banquet masterfully arranged by the Lover of our souls. Pull up a chair. I'm convinced this will be a bountiful buffet. *His Word always is*, and, if you're anything like me, turning down good eatin' has never been an option.

I've wondered how you might react to the subtitle on the cover. That first part—*Your Weakness*—can dig up some deep insecurities. We've all felt feeble, limited, and overwhelmed at one point or another.

Good thing you can't simmer too long on the first half of that subtitle, though, without landing victoriously on the last half—*God's Strength*. I orchestrated it that way. I wanted a quick turnaround from you to Him. From weakness to strength. From impossibility to divine possibility.

This is what it's all about. This is how our needs are all met. This is where our victories are achieved. Your weaknesses don't stand a chance in the face of God's overwhelming, almighty power. In fact, you'll soon see from our study together that He is just waiting to demonstrate to you how your weakness is actually a gift—a key of sorts that unlocks and unleashes His power in your life.

Gideon's going to tell us all about it. So don't be shy. Dig in with both hands and with your whole heart ... until your plate is filled to overflowing.

Ready?

Me too!

Session 1
VIEWER GUIDE

Gideon is among a nation of people who have stopped
_____ _____.

The best way to study a biblical character or book is to observe the
entire _____ in which it is set.

"Then the sons of Israel did _____ _____ _____ in the
sight of the LORD; and the LORD gave them into the hands of Midian
seven years." Judges 6:1

NIV includes the word _____

"In those days there was no king in Israel; everyone did what was right
in his _____ _____." Judges 21:25

God raises up a group of people called _____.

Judges' role: they were _____ by God and _____
by God to _____ the people of God to
_____ the enemies of God.

How and why did God's people who have the favor of God and are
in a covenant relationship with God get to a position of such
_____ and _____?

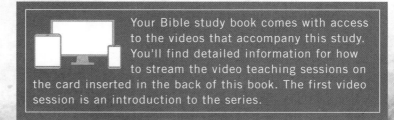

HEADS, HEARTS, AND HANDS

1. They did not know the Lord: there was a problem with the _____ that was in their _____.

a. Their parents didn't do the _____.

b. The _____ people didn't want to _____.

2. There was a problem also with their hearts: their _____ hadn't been stirred for _____ with Him.

3. As a result: their hands aren't _____ the _____ thing.

week
one

GOD'S PEOPLE IN PARADISE

Welcome, my friend. So glad you are diving into Gideon with me. The waters are deep, but the surprises we'll find as we plunge below the surface of this well-loved story will be worth it.

Gideon surprised me, and I think you'll have a similar experience as we turn these pages together. His encounter with God, his responses to God, and his mission from God have struck me right between my spiritual eyes. Turns out there's a lot more happening here than just the underdog drama with Gideon's 300 soldiers and the fleece he laid out under a night sky in hopes of absorbing the will of God.

Gideon's story is much bigger than ... well ... Gideon. Like everything else in the Bible, his story is actually about God and His people. It tells of His love for them, His enduring and boundless mercy toward them, and His strength operating in spite of—even through—weakness in them. And because God's people include you and me, Gideon's story is also about *us*—our lives, our doubts, our struggles, and our possibilities as believers.

From your study or our video session, see if you can recall the answers to the following questions:

How many Bible chapters tell Gideon's story?

GIDEON

This story is bigger
than Gideon.
#LessonsFromGideon

In which book of the Bible are these chapters found?

Since Gideon's story is only a small slice of a 66-book
series, what does this tell us about his story?

As I mentioned during our first video session, understanding the greater
context of Gideon's story and how we fit into it is critical. Unearthing
details about Israel's rich heritage will help us grasp the full weight of his
story. Before we can take home Gideon's lessons, we must identify with
and learn from his people—God's people, Israel.

So journey with me into ancient Israelite territory for a look at how God
sovereignly positioned His man Gideon and what that means for us as He
unfolds our part in His story.

TROUBLE IN PARADISE

When the curtain opens on Gideon and his countrymen in Judges 6,
Israel's brutal 400-year stint of slavery in Egypt is far in the past, as are
their years of wandering in the wilderness. Joshua's military conquests
from a previous century have nestled them deep in the heart of Canaan,
a land "flowing with milk and honey" (a symbolic phrase depicting God's
continuous provision and favor). They are right where Yahweh intended
them to be all along: poised and positioned for His blessing

This ... was paradise.

But Israel's experience in Gideon's day reveals a stunning reality: *we can
spoil paradise and ruin God's abundant blessing.* And the quickest, most surefire
way to do it is to forget the One who gave us the blessing and victory in the
first place.

Gideon and his people are suffering from this lapse in memory. They
have become enthralled with the promised land and have disregarded the
Promise Giver—a mind-set clearly seen in their neglect of God's commands.

Based on Deuteronomy 7:1-2, describe the orders God
had given them in settling the land.

Read the following verses from Judges 1. Draw a line
to connect each verse with the tribe mentioned:

10

Asher	verse 21
Ephraim	verse 27
Benjamin	verse 29
Naphtali	verse 30
Zebulun	verse 31
Manasseh	verse 33

Turn to the map on page 192 and note the territory in Canaan that remained unclaimed by God's people.

One reason the Israelites disobeyed God's command was their fear of the "iron chariots" employed by some of their enemies (Judg. 1:19). The Israelites' military prowess was primitive compared to the Canaanites', who had mastered and kept secret the art of iron production.

With no sophisticated weaponry to match that of the opposing nations, Israel had fared well only when fighting by infantry on foot, especially in the hill country where the terrain kept the enemy's chariots from functioning effectively. Yet God had called them to claim every portion of the land—even the flatland—not just the mountainous territory where victory would come more easily.

Israel was making decisions based on their limited supplies instead of on the boundless resources of their God. If God had commanded their enemies' destruction, He had also taken into account their iron chariots and had planned to equip His people for victory regardless. No weapon could stand against the power of Yahweh. If only Israel had believed that and lived according to it.

If only you and I would do the same.

What, if any, are the "iron chariots" of intimidation that keep you from moving forward in complete obedience to God's Word?

It can be difficult to make sense of Yahweh's command to annihilate an entire people group. Yet He had delayed justice for their rebellion for centuries before sovereignly deeming their cup of iniquity full (Gen. 15:16) and releasing a divine judgment of extermination. The conservation of His people and His redemptive plan was a sign of His desire to show mercy.

Read Psalm 20:7 in the margin and rewrite it in your words and in light of your circumstances.

Some boast in chariots and some in horses, but we will boast in the name of the LORD, our God.
Psalm 20:7

SETTLING TOO SOON

The Israelites thought having access to *some* of the promised land was better than having to fight for *all* of it. So, comfortable and complacent, they chose to enjoy the relative quiet rather than risk upsetting their equilibrium by obeying God completely. They had every right to all of the land—in fact, they already owned it—but since they chose not to possess it, they weren't able to enjoy it.

They chose comfort instead of commitment to the One who had rescued and sustained them—and had promised to continue doing so if they would actively trust Him for total victory. Consider the Deliverance Principle described in the margin. This standard is not specific only to ancient Israel; it's true of us today as we relate to God.

The Deliverance Principle: the one who delivers people from injustice reserves the right to rule over the delivered. The delivered ones become "vassals" and the deliverer is the "suzerain." See Digging Deeper I on page 15.

Describe what the Deliverance Principle should look like in your life. Use Digging Deeper I on page 15 and Deuteronomy 10:12-13 to help.

Partial obedience is always a temptation. Our shortsightedness often makes partial obedience appear to be the best, safest, most reasonable choice, but it always leads to future hardship, eventually making our lives more difficult than they need to be.

Israel's lack of trust in Yahweh and disobedience to His commands brought the dire consequences chronicled in the book of the Bible we will study during these seven weeks.

Use this workbook as an honest journal between you and God. Are you partially obeying God in any area? If so, record the details.

What comforts or perceived sense of security would you need to abandon to fully obey God's instructions?

PARTIALLY IN PARADISE

One of the most prominent effects of Israel's refusal to fully obey was its continuing spiritual decline. Because of the idolatrous influences of its neighbors, Israel found it increasingly difficult to commit to worshipping God. Spiritually, they slipped into the religious patterns of their neighbors, specifically Baal worship. Militarily, they were constantly threatened by surrounding enemies. Between the moral decay and military danger, God's people were weakening spiritually and physically.

From the previous paragraph, list two of the effects of Israel's disobedience.

1.

2.

Can you point to two areas where disobedience might be having a negative, weakening effect on your life? If so, label and describe them.

1.

2.

Had Israel destroyed Canaan's inhabitants as instructed, the ungodly influence and infiltration of idolatry would have all but evaporated. Had there been no enemies left in their territory, the Israelites could have settled into the enjoyment of God's promised land instead of facing extended struggle and oppression from their neighbors.

Are you facing any battles today due to something
you didn't destroy earlier?

When God's Spirit asks us to eliminate something from our lives, we
shouldn't play around with His direction. He sees the future effects of
leftover enemies. Take Him seriously. Fully engage in the task at hand.

As we begin our journey into the life of Gideon, we meet a nation
marked by weakness and decline, living in a time described in one simple yet
powerful way: "Everyone did what was right in his own eyes" (Judg. 21:25).

Maybe this study meets you in the same place: emotionally weakened,
physically exhausted, and spiritually deflated. Maybe you are all too familiar
with the results of a life lived by standards out of alignment with God's.
Don't despair. Good news awaits ahead.

An unsuspecting hero is coming to Israel ... and to you.

At the end of each lesson, I want you to record any
"hashtag" statements that will help you easily recall
what God is teaching you. Remember, you don't have
to be brilliant and incisive; just be led by God's Spirit
on how the lessons apply to you. If you're up for it,
I'd love to see your notes on Twitter followed by the
#LessonsFromGideon label.

Today my #LessonsFromGideon are:

THE DELIVERANCE PRINCIPLE

In the ancient Near East, people sealed relationships between individuals or nations by covenant. When larger, powerful nations and smaller, weaker ones made a covenant, the entities operated like father and son or master and servant. Each had a distinct role to perform.

The more powerful kingdom (called the suzerain) would adopt the smaller one (the vassal). In exchange for the vassal's allegiance, the suzerain would provide military protection and financial provision in times of need. The suzerain had authority over the vassal. It might allow the vassal to maintain its own government and traditions, but it maintained legal ownership of the vassal's land and agricultural harvest.

The vassal was expected to operate in submission to its suzerain. In addition giving a percentage of its annual production, the vassal was expected to be completely loyal. A vassal could only have one suzerain. Making a covenant with another suzerain was high treason and would incur horrendous consequences. The vassal's loyalty was pledged to the suzerain and could not be shared with another.

The Bible translates this kind of loyalty using the Hebrew word *hesed*. It means love, faithfulness, or covenantal faithfulness. A vassal's faithfulness was described as love expressed to his suzerain. Rebellion was to hate the suzerain.

When Yahweh made Israel a nation through Abraham, He used a means people in that era would understand. He cut a covenant. Yahweh became their Suzerain, offering them His unfailing protection and ongoing provision in exchange for the *hesed* of the vassal. They were to have no other suzerains.

God demanded they love the Lord their God "with all their heart, soul, and strength" (Deut. 6:5) not as a passive emotion but as an active condition of their covenant. They were to submit in loyalty to the covenant they had established with Yahweh.

In Gideon's story, Yahweh reminds His vassal of their agreement—He had delivered them from Egypt (Judg. 6:9-10). He provided them with protection and provision as His vassal nation. Israel had failed to fulfill their part of the bargain. They turned to idols and cut covenant with foreign gods, splitting their allegiance when it should have been solely focused on Him. They had committed divine treason against their faithful suzerain.

Treason demanded dire consequences for a vassal, including destruction of his family, land, and even his own life. Yahweh breaks the pattern and extends mercy to Israel despite their failure to remain committed to Him. This mercy was in stark contrast to their cultural experiences. It presented an intriguing lesson to them about their God.

YOU AGAIN?

Fruit flies. They were swarming around the fruit bowl when my family and I returned from a weeklong trip. Before we'd left, I'd worked hard to clean out the refrigerator, removing foods that might spoil while we were away, but I'd completely forgotten the fruit bowl in the center of our kitchen table. Now we would pay the price. The pesky flies were everywhere, and even after the spoiled fruit was put into a trash bag and discarded on the curb, the flies lingered. Getting rid of them after they'd had an uninterrupted vacation in our home was quite a chore.

The Israelites had compromised their ability to fully enjoy the promises of God and remain strong under His canopy of protection and provision. The negative effects of their halfhearted obedience were swarming like fruit flies all around them. This pattern of disobedience was not new to their generation. It was simply a continuation of the cycle started by ancestors who had also disregarded compliance to God's commands. The pesky pagan neighbors of Gideon's era weren't a new development. They'd been there all along. And getting rid of them would not be easy.

> **Is there a problem you're contending with today that's an extension of a difficulty someone else (perhaps in your family line) didn't fully conquer in the past?**

The archenemy Israel will face in this particular segment of Scripture is Midian. The Midianites were a fierce, nomadic tribe who made their homes anywhere they could plunder, rob, and subdue local inhabitants.

While a large portion of this people group moved from place to place, some of them dwelled in cities in the vicinity of Moab. They were a wealthy people whose caravans were considered the "ships of the desert,"[1] traveling back and forth across the arid landscape with valuable spices and other cargo. It was one of these caravans that purchased young Joseph from his conniving brothers several centuries earlier (Gen. 37:28).

The Midianites were distant relatives of the Hebrews. The nation of Israel descended through Isaac, the promised seed, while Midian descended from Isaac's half-brother, Midian, son of Abraham's concubine Keturah (Gen. 25:1).

Look over Abraham's family tree below. Note his descendants through Keturah. Circle Abraham, Keturah, and Midian.

ABRAHAM'S FAMILY TREE

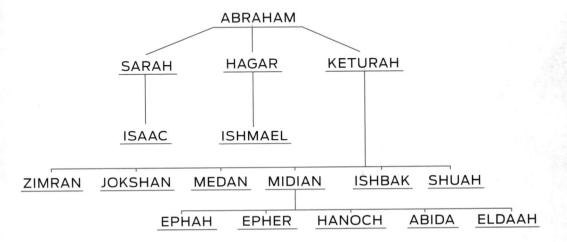

SLEEPING WITH THE ENEMY

A closer look at the Midianites reveals a time of distant friendship between the two people groups. Moses, for example, fled to Midian to escape Pharaoh's wrath (Exod. 2:15) and was taken in by a Kenite (a tribe of Midian) priest. He married one of the priest's daughters, Zipporah, and then shepherded his father-in-law's flocks in the desert of Horeb for forty years. God spoke to Moses from a burning bush while he was tending these flocks.

Moses later invited this Midianite priest-prince, Jethro, to join Israel's journey to the promised land. Many of Jethro's people accompanied them. The Lord's acts during the wilderness journey began to sway these pagan people toward a belief in Yahweh (Exod. 18:10-12). But the influence was soon stunted, and the Midianites became a primary corrupter of Israel.

GIDEON

Today's difficulties are often a result of yesterday's disobedience. #LessonsFromGideon

In the margin, take note of the encounters between Israel and Midian all the way back to the time of Abraham. Put an asterisk beside any unfamiliar scenarios and take time to study them when you can.

Why the history lesson? It may help us interpret the Hebrews' response to God's instructions near Moses' death concerning Midian and the persistence of Israel's troubles with Midian until Gideon's day.

What did God tell Moses in Numbers 31:1-5?

What did Israel do in response to this command (Num. 31:7-15)? Select all that apply.
☐ slaughtered all the males
☐ spared the women and children
☐ killed the kings
☐ plundered the city and took the spoils

Of the option(s) you chose, which violated God's command (verse 15)?

How might Israel's initial relationship with Midian have played a part in Israel partially obeying God's instructions?

The divine mandate to annihilate the Midianites was carried out incompletely. The pattern of halfhearted obedience when dealing with enemies seems embedded into the Hebrew psyche. Moses sought to rectify the people's actions by commanding that everyone except the virgin girls be killed. But the small remnant, along with the nomadic Midianite population, was apparently enough to reinvent this tribe of fierce people who sought vengeance on Israel later. When that day came, the Midianites were as thick as "a swarm of locusts" (Judg. 7:12, HCSB), terrorizing God's people.

As far as we can tell from Scripture, Moses acted on God's orders, but the Hebrews were marked even in these early days by an unwillingness to completely obey God. Their penchant for leaving God's business half done created a ripple of consequences for God's people. What a sobering thought to consider: yesterday's partial obedience creates staggering consequences in today's experiences.

Consider this question again in light of what you are learning today: Is there anything God is leading you to completely "annihilate" in your life that may once have been healthy but is now unhealthy?

Feeling hesitant to follow through on God's instructions? Describe any past connections with the relationship/activity that make it difficult for you to completely end it.

For Group Discussion: Note the number of Midianite girls left alive in Moses' day (Num. 31:35) and the number of Israel's troops gathered to combat the Midianites in Gideon's day (Judg. 7:3). Do you see any significance in this similarity?

More than 150 years after Moses, Israel was facing the same enemy as before who, according to Judges 6, wreaked havoc on them—destroying their crops and livestock. Like fruit flies left in rotten fruit, the Midianites weren't going to be easily eliminated. The question was whether God's people would seek His direction and heed His instructions. This was not the only time in history when the Israelites disobeyed God's initial instruction to destroy an enemy and then faced the resurgence of that enemy.

The Old Testament is a vast collection of data and dates that can easily run together into one long, confusing package. For a better understanding of our study time line, see Digging Deeper II on page 21.

Read 1 Samuel 15:1-9; 30:1-3. Then write 3 to 5 sentences about Israel's experience with the Amalekites. Answer these questions in your writing.

- What did God command His people to do?
- How did they respond?
- What effect did the Amalekites have on Israel later on?

_____

_____

_____

_____

FRESH START

My friend Erin comes from a lineage of folks who have made poor fiscal choices. She can tell stories of massive financial mismanagement, over-spending, and even theft. Her generation is still dealing with the debris.

Maybe your story is similar to Erin's and you're struggling with some-thing your parents or grandparents refused to handle appropriately in their time. Your life may be harder and less manageable than it would have been had they been more alert, responsible, and faithful to godly standards. Or maybe God is asking *you* to break ties with something for the sake of those who will follow in your family.

Israel can relate to you in either case: although their trouble with Midian began generations earlier, they were about to receive a holy summons to start fresh and build a new legacy. They were not to wallow in their ancestors' mishaps or continue their rebellion. This was a brand new day and Yahweh's grace was on a brand new mission. No matter their history, the Israelites had a God who would raise up an individual to change the tide of His people. In their day it was Gideon.

I wonder if, in this day, it's you.

End today's lesson in prayer, using the space below to record any "hashtag" statements God brings to mind. Ask Him to reveal any resentment you may have from others' failures that have brought needless hardship into your life and to give you the courage to forgive. Ask Him to give you the spiritual sensitivity to hear His call and to obey Him completely. Then choose to make today's decisions with tomorrow in mind.

Today my #LessonsFromGideon are:

OLD TESTAMENT TIME LINE

Taking time to familiarize yourself with the progression from Abraham to the time that the judges ruled will be well worth the effort, my friend. It will help you understand not only Gideon's story but the entire Bible. So grab a latte and spend a few minutes looking over the time line below. As you do, think of other Bible characters and events you are familiar with from the Old Testament and how they fit into the time line. Don't rush. Take your time and absorb the details.

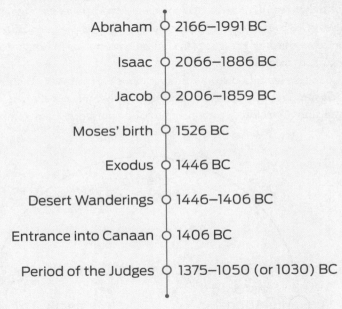

Abraham	2166–1991 BC
Isaac	2066–1886 BC
Jacob	2006–1859 BC
Moses' birth	1526 BC
Exodus	1446 BC
Desert Wanderings	1446–1406 BC
Entrance into Canaan	1406 BC
Period of the Judges	1375–1050 (or 1030) BC

Note that scholars hold differing opinions about some of these dates. Don't be bothered if you find variations in resources. This list gives you a sense of the period of the time involved.

Now look at the time line below. Mark the date of Abraham's era and the era of the judges on the following time line. You can reference this page throughout your study.

2500 BC	2000 BC	1500 BC	1000 BC

GOD'S STORY, MY STORY

I'm so glad you've hung in there for this study into Israel's history. The most accurate way to interpret Scripture is by viewing a passage and its characters through the overarching historical and covenantal grid of that particular book. Having a framework into which you can lodge all your biblical data helps you better understand how everything fits together.

In light of that framework, consider this: *the main message of the entire Bible is God's redemption of humanity.* From beginning to end, Scripture spells out the divine rescue plan God is orchestrating to bring people back into relationship with Himself.

God's redemption story contains a four-part pattern: (1) rejection of God's way, (2) decline of God's people, (3) consequences allowed by God's hand, and (4) restored relationship to God's presence. Think of it as a cycle.

To see one of the redemption cycles play out in Scripture, read Judges 2:11 (rejection), 2:14 (decline and consequences), and 2:16 (restoration).

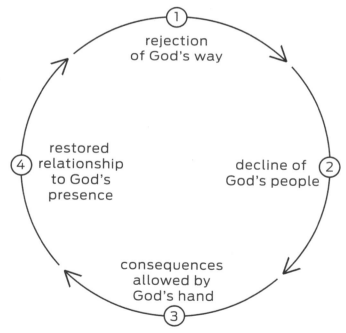

① rejection of God's way

② decline of God's people

③ consequences allowed by God's hand

④ restored relationship to God's presence

Describe the cycle of redemption in your own words.

This pattern happens again and again in different time periods, involving different people. Scholars are fairly unified in identifying three major instances of the pattern.

- The first redemption cycle was during the antediluvian (pre-flood) period of history from the time of Adam until that of Noah.
- The second cycle began after the flood and concluded during the time of Daniel and Ezra.
- The third began after the exile in Babylon with the rebuilding of the temple under Ezra and culminated in the creation of the Church in the New Testament.

One, two, three. Three different cycles but each with the same divine purpose: *the redemption of God's people*. Since we are a part of His Church, you and I are an important part of this plan. We are players in God's grand redemption story.

The overarching message of the Bible is _____ _____.

Complete the three cycles of redemption seen in the Scriptures:

Redemption Cycle #1. From Adam to _____

Redemption Cycle #2. Post-flood to the time of _____ and _____.

Redemption Cycle #3. Rebuilding the _____ under the leadership of _____ to the conception of the _____.

I, _____(your name), am a part of the grand story of redemption seen in the Bible.

THE JUDGES

Now let's drill down to locate Gideon's position on this larger biblical landscape. The Book of Judges sits within the second cycle in your list— the historical era between the flood and Israel's exile in Babylon. Deeper

If you had to pinpoint where you fall in this cycle right now, where would it be and why? Write your name beside that portion of the cycle.

Then the LORD raised up judges who delivered them from the hands of those who plundered them.
Judges 2:16

within that second cycle, the stories in Judges are specifically situated in the "decline" and "consequence" stages. God's appointment of judges was designed to coax the people toward "restoration."

Flip back to the redemption cycle chart on page 22. Write "The Judges/Gideon" near "decline" and "consequence" portions of Israel's history. What adjectives would you use to describe the state of the Israelites during this stage (Judg. 6:1-6)?

If you had to choose a stage in the cycle to define your community right now, which would it be? Write it in the appropriate place on the cycle on page 22. What adjectives would you use to describe your own community right now?

This was one of the most feeble, pathetic, and unbecoming seasons in the life of God's people. During this time, divine judgment was warranted. One look at the people's inconsistency, their forgetfulness and ingratitude, their reckless disobedience, and their rejection of God reveals that they fully deserved the oppression and punishment that was coming to them.

Yet ... because of God's covenant, mercy prevailed. He judged His people only to restore and reconcile them, so the cycle of redemption could continue and His story could be told. The fact that this cycle continues today—despite the ongoing obstinacy of fallen humanity—speaks of His right-this-minute desire to extend mercy and redeem people. Even now.

What are some of the signs that reveal God's mercy for our culture today?

What does Judges 2:18 reveal about the heart of God for His people, even when they're suffering the rightful consequences of their sin?

TURNING POINTS

Yesterday, you looked at the time line of Israel's history. Many biblical characters we admire represent God's intersection with the Hebrews' experience during the "decline" or "consequence" stage of the redemption cycle. The great heroes of the Bible didn't appear at the zenith of their cultures, but at the low points as part of God's effort to rescue and redirect His people back to the covering of His covenant. Consider the following:

- After the fall of Adam, Yahweh used Abraham to create a nation who would always be holy unto Himself.
- When the Israelites were enslaved in Egypt, He raised up Moses to deliver them to a land flowing with God's protection and provision.
- When they were oppressed by their enemies in this promised land, Yahweh raised up judges to be His representatives and lead the people out from under enemy subjugation.

Through each stage of Israel's experience, God invaded the human experience with His restoring, preserving activity. If I were with you, I'd give you a high-five in celebration of God's unending mercy and graciousness!

On the time line at the bottom of page 21 write "Redemption Story" as the title.

You and I are a part of the divine story of redemption just as much as any other person listed on the time line. Even as God empowered each of these to do unique things on His behalf in their generation, so you and I, as a part of His Church, have been commissioned to rise up in our own way to serve His purposes in our generation. Your involvement in this study may show that He's stirring something in you right now.

One reason I believe the Lord led me to Gideon's story and has now brought us into this study together is to remind us of the significance of His unique calling. As mothers to our children, as employees in the workplace, as part of His body in our local church, or as influencers in our communities, God has deliberately positioned each of us to be His representative, beckoning our ailing culture to Him—one person at a time. Yes, our calling will look different from Moses' and Gideon's. We will probably not be leading pilgrims out of bondage or troops into battle. But no matter what God's plan looks like in our lives, His hand is on us to wage war against the enemy within our spheres of influence.

The most important way God has reminded me to do this is through rearing my children. I'm convinced that God lets me witness their cute, comical lives to give me good material in my teaching. But without a doubt, outside of my relationship with the Lord and my husband, my sons are my highest priority, and I have been commissioned by God to be their mother. Being a parent may seem like a commonplace human relationship, but I will not be lulled into downplaying it as ordinary. My role as a mom is a deliberate strategy initiated by God to rear young boys into godly men. And I am resolved to fulfill this calling—to be for them what God needs me to be during this critical stage in their lives.

Your assignment may look different from mine, but neither takes second place to that of Abraham, Moses, Deborah, or Gideon. God will empower us to complete His work, multiplying our simple efforts to achieve maximum results. Wherever we feel too weak to fulfill our calling, our ever-redeeming God will make us strong!

> What realm of life do you think God wants you concentrating on while doing this study? Don't overlook the ordinary or minimize your role in a larger arena. Let Him lead your thinking and trust Him to equip you for whatever He inspires.

Israel's culture during the time of the judges is not much different from our own. Sin runs rampant and morality continues to decline. He is still searching, not for perfect people, but for individuals who are passionate about Him and committed to His call on their lives.

Recommit yourself to God's assignment in this season. Ask the Lord to open your eyes to recognize His purpose for you in His story of redemption. Also, take time to lift up your community and country to the Lord. Ask Him to stir conviction and draw people back to Himself.

Today my #LessonsFromGideon are:

DAY 4
EMPOWERED TO ACT

My son was frustrated this morning because his handheld video game unit kept powering down every few seconds. He'd push the power button and the screen would light up for ten to fifteen seconds, then go black again. He brought it to me, upset and irritated that his little machine was causing him such big problems. I asked him the same question I want to ask you: *Did you charge it up?*

Scripture outlines the faults of the judges in great detail. Samson, for instance, is almost more known for his salacious appetite and hot temper than his brave feats. Scripture makes no attempt to hide the frailty of these leaders, allowing us to clearly recognize the strengthening effect God's Spirit can have on anyone to accomplish God's tasks. Apart from His Spirit, these judges could not have functioned with any sort of effectiveness.

Neither can we. This is one of the most important lessons to learn from the period during which the judges ruled Israel.

> We have nothing going for us except what God puts into us.
> #LessonsFromGideon

Fill in the blanks below from our Week 1 video session.
Use your hand movements if it helps you remember.
(For a reminder, see page 181 for an explanation.)

The judges were _____ by God and then _____ by God to _____ the people of God for the purpose of _____ _____ the enemies of God.

Note the following chart of the judges, the reference for their stories, the oppressor they faced, their identifying characteristics, and lengths of their service. Some scholars list twelve judges while others name up to sixteen. Neither way of numbering the judges is incorrect, but the higher number comes from including other prominent men in Israel like Samuel and Eli. For the purposes of our study, we have highlighted only those who bear the Hebrew title *shaphat,* which means "to judge."

GIDEON

Judge	Reference	Oppressor	Identifying Attributes	Length of Time
Othniel	3:7-11	Mesopotamian	fierce and dominating in war	40 years
Ehud	3:12-30	Moabites	peacemaker, fearless, intolerant of sin	80 years
Shamgar	3:31	Philistines	resourceful and creative	years not specified
Deborah	4–5	Canaanites	patient, bold, fearless	40+ years
Gideon	6–8	Midianites	weak, questioning, scared, nervous	40 years
Tola	10:1-2	not named	no description	23 years
Jair	10:3-5	not named	resourceful and vain	22 years
Jephthah	11–12:7	Ammonites	an illegitimate son, kicked out of his own home	6 years
Ibzan	12:8-10	not named	no description	7 years
Elon	12:11-12	not named	no description	10 years
Abdon	12:13-15	not named	vain	8 years
Samson	13–16	Philistines	morally weak, physically strong	20 years

Look up at least two of the following verses and record the common theme shared between them:

☐ Judges 2:18   ☐ Judges 11:29

☐ Judges 3:10   ☐ Judges 13:25

☐ Judges 6:34

Judges in this era were not like our modern-day judges who arbitrate in a court of law. The primary purpose of an Old Testament judge was to relieve military pressure on the tribes of Israel and deliver them from the oppression of foreign nations. God handpicked people for the job who were terribly flawed, then empowered them to fulfill these roles in spite of their shortcomings. He chose them from circles that would have seemed inappropriate to observers. Such is God's way, selecting "what is foolish in the world to shame the wise and ... what is weak in the world to shame the strong" (1 Cor. 1:27).

As the fifth judge, Gideon was far from perfect. In fact, Gideon's story doesn't even end triumphantly. But God used Gideon to reinvigorate His people during a time of great despair and discouragement.

As 1 Corinthians 10:6 reminds us, the Old Testament record serves as an example for us. Principles unearthed from the ancient record give counsel to us today. With that in mind, here are three functions of the judges to consider in light of your life. We'll look at each one briefly. The judges served to (1) unify the people of God, (2) fight against the oppression of the enemy, and (3) operate by the empowerment of God's Spirit.

What connections do you see between the judges' role in the Old Testament and the role of modern believers as members of the family of God? Use the references in the margin for guidance if necessary.

Yesterday you pinpointed an assignment to which God is calling you. Which one of the above roles would be the most difficult for you in that task? Why?

Behold, how good and how pleasant it is for brothers to dwell together in unity!
Psalm 133:1

For our struggle is not against flesh and blood, but against ... the spiritual forces of wickedness in the heavenly places.
Ephesians 6:12

I am filled with power—with the Spirit of the LORD.
Micah 3:8

PRESERVING UNITY

Israel was weakened both spiritually and militarily. One sign of this weakness was their isolation from each other. While Yahweh had rallied the Hebrews into one nation at Sinai years earlier, they now lived separate, disconnected lives.

Fighting the enemy successfully required a joint effort among the tribes, and a divinely appointed judge was needed to glue them together. In Gideon's case, Israel's troops would rally at the first sound of his trumpet. All of the troops that were called would rush to assist him in his efforts to stand against Midian.

Unity does not mean sameness. It means oneness of purpose.
#LessonsFromGideon

How do you think the church fares today in being one body of believers? Think of specific examples to support evidence for or against this goal.

Be completely humble and gentle; be patient, bearing with one another in love. Make every effort to keep the unity of the Spirit through the bond of peace.
Ephesians 4:2-3, NIV

According to the passage from Ephesians in the margin, what are the four attributes necessary in helping maintain harmony and accord among believers? I've added an attribute that I think is implied in the second portion of the passage.

1.

2.

3.

4. Persistence

Circle the attribute you think is most lacking in the divisive situations you've experienced.

Which one of these is the hardest for you to maintain right now? Why?

Supposedly, the most segregated hour in America is on Sunday morning when Christians gather for church, divided along lines of denomination, culture, race, and worship style. And though often unintentional, this separation keeps the strength of the global church from flourishing against the cultural attacks of the enemy.

This epidemic of disunity plagues not only our churches but, even more detrimentally, our own homes. Many husbands and wives are divided in their purpose, and children are estranged from their parents. These fissures leave families exposed to enemy fire.

For Group Discussion:
Brainstorm creative ways to foster and maintain unity in your family, your church, and your Bible study group.

WAGING WAR

Like it or not, spiritual warfare exists. We may never take up arms with a shield and sword like Gideon, but we are no less in a battle every day. We know it. We feel it. Victory requires constant effort to take "every thought captive to the obedience of Christ" (2 Cor. 10:5). By God's Spirit, we can be successful—the same way the judges were. Only through God's supernatural empowerment were they able to deliver the people out of oppression and into Yahweh's freedom and governance. Whether or not the judges were effective at their job was determined by whether or not the enemy was still effective at his.

So take inventory:
Does the enemy have to think twice about his schemes against your family because of your watchful presence? Why or why not?

Do the enemy's attempts become quickly thwarted because you are alert and prayerful?

Are you on guard and aware of the spiritual nature behind physical events in your life?

Your thoughtful, prayerful responses to these questions will enable you to become better prepared to take up your position each day against the insidious, unseen forces at work against victory in Christ.

STAYING EMPOWERED

The bottom line is that empowerment by God's Spirit is a necessity for success. Supernatural acts require supernatural equipping. If we haven't been charged up, we can't expect to operate correctly any more than my little boy could expect his toy to function properly without being plugged in. Both need to be connected and refueled to serve their purposes.

And when they are?

Game on!

Unifying the tribes of Israel and leading them to victory against foreign nations would be an enormous task for any human being. Yet because judges like Gideon were empowered by God's Spirit, they could lead in spite of themselves. Now, because of Jesus, a greater anointing by the Holy Spirit is available to you and me. If you are a believer in Christ, you already have access to the strength the Spirit gives simply because He lives in you.

Having also believed, you were sealed in Him with the Holy Spirit of promise.

Ephesians 1:13

Paul prayed that God, by His power, would fulfill "every desire for goodness and the work of faith" (2 Thess. 1:11). If you are discouraged today, even brokenhearted because of failures or a lack of desire to stand strong in battle, ask the Lord to renew your passion, bolster your confidence in Him, and establish you in the work He's called you to do.

Today my #LessonsFromGideon are:

DAY 5
TURNING THE TIDE

Visiting my paternal grandparents is a nostalgic adventure with sights, smells, and sounds that transport me back to my childhood. This husband and wife, married for sixty-two years, are in love with each other in that sickeningly wonderful way that brings a smile to your face. They still live in the same row house where they raised my father and his siblings. And while their home sits in a drug-infested neighborhood in Baltimore, it is somehow a safe haven of peace and security for all who enter.

When I walked in for a visit yesterday, I grinned at the sight of the old piano I used to play as a girl while sitting on my grandfather's knee; the plastic-covered sofa my sweaty legs always stuck to in the heat of summer; the pictures, signs, and banners that lined their walls with declarations of a deep faith and love for the Lord.

I poked around in my grandparent's basement during my visit and uncovered this treasure. It brought tears to my eyes to see my precious grandfather and me together nearly 40 years ago. He's loved me well for a long time.

On one of those placards are words I remember hearing quite often from my grandparents' lips during our summer visits: "As for me and my house, we will serve the LORD" (Josh. 24:15).

In the margin record a few key notes about how Joshua's generation had responded to Joshua's appeal (Josh. 24:16-24).

GIDEON

Back in Joshua's day and through the time of the judges, the blessings and bounty of divine favor were always available to God's people when they honored this "me and my house" commitment of faithfulness to the Lord. In our study this week, we've seen how within the span of one generation they had tumbled down a slippery slope of moral decay and landed in a pool of national disaster.

What were two primary reasons Israel was faltering? (Judg. 2:10)

1.

2.

If you've noticed spiritual apathy in your own life, which of the above options do you feel has contributed most to this?

CIRCLING BACK

Our Bible study this week has been intense but rich, hasn't it? Granted, the bumpy terrain of Israel's history required us to abandon our cute convertibles for intense four-wheel-drive SUVs of persistence. But we've made it to the end of our first week together. Now let's circle back to consider what we've studied and make our own resolutions.

The people in Gideon's generation were facing difficulties as a result of parents and grandparents who had failed to pass on the baton of faith. Or, if they had, this younger generation had not received it well, ignoring what could have been the key to their future spiritual success.

For lack of guidance a nation falls, but victory is won through many advisers.
Proverbs 11:14, NIV

From the previous paragraph, underline the two possible reasons for the nation's lack of knowledge about God.

Which one of these do you think has been the most central to moral decline in our day? Why? Be prepared to discuss your reasoning with your group.

When we see spiritual apathy growing in ourselves and others, it's time to figure out why. Then our goal must be to flesh out the truths of God's Word, open ourselves to His activity in our daily lives, learn from those who are doing it well, and seek to inspire others through our example.

> Take a moment to respond to the following questions.
>
> 1. Who are some younger people you can be intentional about teaching?
>
> 2. How can you creatively share the truth of God with them?
>
> 3. Do you have a teachable spirit that is ready and willing to receive lessons learned from more seasoned saints?
>
> 4. How can you deliberately position yourself to learn?

At most stages in our lives, we are in two roles at the same time: both the younger and the older generation, because there are always sisters older and younger than we are. Circle the category you normally plug yourself into. Now consider how you can be strategic about putting yourself in the other category this week.

CAPTAIN OF MY SOUL

Humanism is a man-centered religion running rampant in our world today. It is a theology that places more importance on an individual's rational thought than on adherence to religious principle. Humanists embrace their own reasoning as the basis of their decision making. They may want God, but only on their terms and only if He doesn't clash with their personal sense of rightness and happiness. They want the benefits of a relationship with none of the responsibilities.

Baalism was an ancient form of secular humanism, offering a god that catered to the needs of mankind. Baal and his female consort, Asherah, represented fertility and prosperity to the ancients and did not have a law book like Yahweh's. Fertility and prosperity without rules? The Israelites were

There is a way which seems right to a man, but its end is the way of death.
Proverbs 14:12

sold on it. So they sought to manipulate these idols for personal benefit. Yet as Israel suffered under continuous oppression, it was clear that Baal was ineffective. Year after year, their harvest was stolen and starvation soon set in. Baal was as impotent then as humanism is now.

> **Underline words or key phrases in the previous paragraphs that show the similarities between ancient Baalism and modern humanism. Write any thoughts about these resemblances.**

> **How do you see this verse demonstrated in modern humanistic tendencies? "In those days there was no king in Israel; everyone did what was right in his own eyes" (Judg. 21:25).**

We easily overlook the personal significance of Baalism. This kind of lifestyle can seem foreign to us. After all, we don't use words like "idol" or "Asherah" in our everyday conversation.

You're probably thinking, "Priscilla, I'm not a humanist!" But consider this: Can you name a prior conviction you've abandoned or compromised, replacing it (even unknowingly) with a standard that's more in line with the philosophies you hear on television or see in the world? Whenever we allow secular perspectives to set the guidelines for our daily consecrated life, we are living—in that one area, at least—a humanistic version of Christianity.

> **In what ways can you detect humanism creeping into Christianity as a whole?**

Only a return to Yahweh could change the tide of famine and humiliation for Israel. And only a recommitment to Yahweh and His standards can reverse the degrading epidemic of today.

God is calling you and me to do our part in turning the tide.

BRAVE

My grandparents' legacy of faith has had an astounding, far-reaching effect on their children, grandchildren, and great-grandchildren. They've chosen to intentionally and strategically stand strong against the tide of untrue doctrine and to honor the God of Abraham, Isaac, and Jacob.

But their legacy could never have existed had they not chosen to start it. Their parents were not Christians. When my grandparents met the Lord in their late twenties, they did an about-face to walk an entirely different life path. They taught the Word in their home and lived it out in front of my father and his siblings. Even today, few minutes pass in their company before they overflow with Scripture and thoughtful conversation about spiritual matters.

As a result of their change, the trajectory of our entire family destiny has altered. The overflow of such deliberate mentoring has been my blessing. How grateful I am for grandparents who were brave enough to turn the tide.

I share this not to cause you sadness if your reality is different, but to encourage you to turn the tide of your legacy if needed. Someone needs to make the change. It may as well be you ... and it may as well be now.

The heading for this section is "brave." In what ways will a holy bravery be required for you to continue or start a legacy of faith?

One generation shall praise Your works to another, and shall declare Your mighty acts.
Psalm 145:4

End this week by prayerfully considering what it will mean to live out Joshua 24:15. Ask the Lord to give you a holy courage to turn this promise into personal reality. When ready, rewrite the words of this verse in a personal way as a commitment to the Lord from this day forward.

Today my #LessonsFromGideon are:

"If it is disagreeable in your sight to serve the Lord, choose for yourselves today whom you will serve: whether the gods which your fathers served which were beyond the River, or the gods of the Amorites in whose land you are living; but as for me and my house, we will serve the Lord."
Joshua 24:15

Session 2
VIEWER GUIDE

DISTINGUISHING CHARACTERISTICS OF THE MIDIANITES:

You know you are dealing with the Midianites when the trouble is coming from the most _____ place.

You know you are dealing with the Midianites because just when you get your _____ above _____, that problem _____ again.

WHAT SHOULD YOU EXPECT WHEN YOU'RE EXPECTING?

1. The crisis is not _____ enough to place you out of the _____ of God.

    Isaiah 59:1

2. The crisis does _____ you for your _____.

    Judges 6:12-13

God is more interested in changing your _____ than He is your _____.

    Luke 19:17

    Hebrews 11:32-34

To access the video teaching sessions, use the instructions in the back of your Bible study book.

WHAT TO EXPECT WHEN YOU'RE EXPECTING

Judges 6:12

No matter how you feel, what the _____ says about you is _____.

1 Peter 2:9

3. Your crisis does not _____ your _____.

Judges 6:11-12, 14

The angel of the Lord _____ (v. 11) , _____ (v. 12), _____ (v. 14).

week
two

COMMISSIONING GIDEON

Yesterday, I walked into my bedroom to grab a book from my bedside table. Sliding past a chair in the corner, I scoured the table for the book. As I turned to leave, I nearly jumped out of my socks when an enormous shadowy figure suddenly moved in the corner.

My husband, all 250 pounds of him, had been sitting in that corner chair the whole time, watching me search. He had seen me, but I hadn't seen him. Not until he started to get up did I even realize he was there.

We have come upon one of the most fascinating parts of the entire narrative: Gideon's encounter with the angel of the Lord.

> Then the angel of the LORD came and sat under the oak that was in Ophrah, which belonged to Joash the Abiezrite as his son Gideon was beating out wheat in the wine press in order to save it from the Midianites. The angel of the LORD appeared to him (Judg. 6:11-12).

Underline the three action verbs connected with "the angel of the LORD" in the passage above.

GIDEON

The angel of the Lord (*Malak Yahweh*) is described by scholar John Marshal Lang as the "Great presence in Israelite History." He was the eternal, pre-existent Christ, and His appearance was one of the astounding theophanies (God-appearances) in the Old Testament. Other appearances of the Malak Yahweh in the Old Testament: Gen. 16:7-13, Exodus 3:2, Numbers 22:22

Ordinary is often the disguise of the divine.
#LessonsFromGideon

I wonder what caused Gideon to become aware of the angel's presence? Did the angel rise from his seated position? Did he make a quick movement that caught Gideon's eye? Did he cough or sniffle, maybe even clear his throat in a slightly sarcastic way?

The Hebrew word translated "appeared" in verse 12 suggests the angel presented himself, making himself visible to Gideon. The angel's actions made it possible for Gideon to see him. Scripture isn't clear as to what brought the angel to Gideon's attention, but the sequence of events is evident. In verse 11, the angel was sitting under the oak tree but not until verse 12 does it say he "appeared" to Gideon.

Whether he had been sitting there for only a few seconds or perhaps for several minutes (or longer) is unclear. But what we can deduce from the text is this: the angel finding Gideon was a separate occurrence from Gideon finding the angel.

This means that probably no lightning strike accompanied the angel's arrival. Nor was he sparkling in a shimmering haze. He wasn't a see-through, floating immortal who hovered inches above the ground, and no flash mob broke into the "Hallelujah Chorus" to herald his arrival. No, this angel most likely had the look of an ordinary man who had come to Gideon in an ordinary way during an ordinary day.

God often comes to us in our "boring" days, veiled in the most ordinary of circumstances. In fact, "ordinary" is often the disguise of the divine. If we are constantly anticipating a grandiose event to accompany the times when we encounter Him or hear His voice, we will miss out on many intimate moments in our relationship with God. The mundane, the routine, the commonplace—these are often the contexts in which He will reveal Himself to humanity.

Having your spiritual radar up in consistent anticipation of His presence—even in the midst of the joyful chaos and regular rhythms of your everyday living— is paramount in hearing God, because sometimes the place and manner you find Him is the least spectacular you'd expect.

Oh, yes, sometimes His presence has made the hair on the back of my neck stand straight up. But more often than not, flashy and flamboyant are not His style. Being mindful of this and recognizing Him even when His glory is shrouded in normalcy is a prerequisite for gaining clarity in your calling. To be aware of God's purpose, you must first be aware of His presence.

What expectations do you think believers have of how God reveals Himself?

How do you think these expectations have been formed?

How might these beliefs keep people from recognizing a God encounter in their lives?

> Knowing God's purpose requires first being aware of God's presence.
> #LessonsFromGideon

SEEING GOD

In Ephesians 1:18-19, Paul records one amazingly long and spiritually rich sentence: "I pray that the eyes of your heart may be enlightened, so that you will know what is the hope of His calling, what are the riches of the glory of His inheritance in the saints, and what is the surpassing greatness of His power toward us who believe."

Fill in the blanks to chart the progression in the verse.

Paul prays that the _____ of their hearts may be _____. The result will be that they will _____ what is the _____ of His _____, the _____ of the glory of His _____, and the surpassing greatness of His _____ for believers.

Now that you've filled in the blanks above, go back and read the statement aloud. Take it in slowly and note the progression from one stage to the next. What summary idea do you take from the text?

GIDEON

Opened eyes precede your calling being realized.

#LessonsFromGideon

Do you see hints of these phases even in Gideon's case? He became aware of God's presence first and then discovered a new calling and the power to accomplish it. The same pattern is true for us. As believers, our spiritual eyes must detect God's presence. Once this happens, the opportunity unfolds for us to understand our calling and the vast inheritance we've been given to accomplish the tasks before us.

We often want to get on with the purposes of God (especially if we think doing so will get us out from under the shadow of the oak tree), forgoing the necessary prefix to that reality—becoming aware of and honoring His presence with us. First the angel caused Gideon to become aware of his nearness, then he spoke God's Word to him.

Consider Samuel's example. Read 1 Samuel 3:4-11.
Then number each statement in chronological order.
☐ Samuel is entrusted with a message from God.
☐ Samuel says, "Speak, LORD, for Your servant is
  listening."
☐ God speaks but Samuel is unaware that it is God.
☐ Samuel's mentor helps him realize that God is
  speaking.

Apparently, God's voice was unaccompanied by pomp and fanfare. In fact, it was so unexciting that it sounded like the voice of an aged man. Had God not persisted, Samuel might not have ever realized that this ordinary voice belonged to an extraordinary Being.

I wonder how often God has been near, but I haven't noticed because I assumed that His nearness would always be coupled with astonishing circumstances.

Today, Gideon's story encourages us to seek the Almighty in the midst of normalcy. Ask the Lord to make Himself visible to you just as He did to Gideon. Pray that He will open your spiritual eyes over the next twenty-four hours so you can see Him more clearly than ever before.

Today my #LessonsFromGideon are:

DAY 2

THRESHING ... AND OTHER ORDINARY THINGS

The plumbers are here today. They've determined the house needs a complete plumbing renovation. The pipes are old, rusted, and leaking everywhere. Everything needs replacing. All of it.

Our plumber is a kind man who has delivered the news as gently as possible. The expense of overhauling the whole system is staggering. Perhaps it was the whites of our eyes or the shortness of our breath that caused him to make the offer, but right after he told us the repair price, he threw in a few extras for free—a couple of new toilets and a new tankless water heater. His reasoning: "All my work is going to be underground. It's always nice to see something happening above the ground too."

He's right. Seeing something change always helps. In fact, if we look at what Gideon was doing when his angelic visitor appeared, we'll see the above-ground evidence of things happening below the surface in his life.

So, today we have a lesson in threshing.

In the margin write anything you know about the purpose and process of threshing.

> Gideon was threshing wheat in a winepress to keep it from the Midianites.
> Judges 6:11, NIV

THRESHING

At this point in the year in Gideon's story, wise farmers could be found threshing—separating the meaty, nutrient-rich grain from the <u>light, airy, and useless chaff.</u> Typically, the wheat harvest would be taken to an open-air station called a threshing floor, where oxen pulling a heavy slab would trample it underfoot. This process yielded a better result in less time than threshing the wheat by hand. Gideon had neither the luxury of taking his harvest to a threshing floor nor the desire to attract the Midianites' attention by doing his threshing in public.

Instead, Gideon was working in a winepress—a small enclosed space—and most likely using a small instrument called a flail (two thick boards fused together, studded with sharp stone fragments on one side) to slowly knock the grain loose from the stalk. Normally only the poor used this method. Imagine Gideon hunched over his stack of wheat, dedicated to the

> For more study: Chaff was often used as imagery for spiritual principles. Here are some examples:
> Psalm 1:4
> Psalm 83:13
> Isaiah 33:11
> Luke 3:17

arduous task of a farmhand. His task was as mundane and necessary for him as washing the dinner dishes might be for you.

List five ordinary tasks you perform on a daily basis.

1.

2.

3.

4.

5.

Think back to the main points in yesterday's lesson. The angel appeared to Gideon in an ordinary way. Yet equally significant is the fact that he appeared while Gideon was doing an ordinary task—threshing wheat.

So, look back to the first paragraph of this section on threshing and underline the word that describes the key purpose of threshing.

SEPARATION

It is interesting that Gideon's name means "hewer, slasher, hacker, cutter."[1]

Raised in an agrarian culture, Gideon had become so accustomed to the routine of threshing that its familiarity may have blinded him to the significance of what God was subtly showing him. Gideon's physical act of separating grain from chaff pointed to his future task.

Turn to Judges 6:25-26 and record the details of the first task that Gideon would be asked to undertake.

From what was God asking Gideon to begin separating Israel?

Gideon was being prepared to separate one nation from another, one kingdom from another, God's people from God's enemies. He would even be called to do some very personal threshing—separating himself from his own allegiance to Baal. Separation was about to become a big part of what God was calling him to do.

I love how Scripture does this—building layer upon layer of meaning into these "routine" biblical events. Remember, this is God's story; not just Gideon's. Even in the mundane detail of this timid farmer's experience, God was grooming him for his calling and for the separating process He was about to initiate with His people. This was not just a man threshing wheat; it was God painting some above-ground imagery for Gideon (and us) to see.

If we'll look around, we might also find Him preparing us as He works through our daily lives. Today's tasks—even the most mundane of them—are often preparation for tomorrow's calling. They can carry clues to what He is leading us to learn and accomplish as we faithfully serve Him.

While it might seem comical to find spiritual principles in washing dishes or answering phones at your desk job, God is teaching you faithfulness, diligence, and integrity through every task.

Take a minute to pray. Ask the Lord to reveal a specific spiritual lesson He might be teaching you through one of the tasks you listed at the beginning of today's lesson. Record them as He reveals them.

> Today's tasks are preparation for tomorrow's calling.
> #LessonsFromGideon

UNSEEN ABUNDANCE

Separation was not the only thing God was communicating to Gideon through threshing. Based on what we know of the Israelites' ordeal at the time, it's hard to picture them as being fruitful, underline{abundant, and prosperous}. But the ordinary task of threshing sheds an interesting light on an easily overlooked perspective.

> Gideon would name his firstborn son Jether, which means "abundance."[2]

> **Look up the following passages. What connection do both make between God's faithfulness and threshing?**
>
> Leviticus 26:3-5
>
> Joel 2:24

These verses describe a full threshing floor, overrun with a harvest resulting from God's favor. Threshing, in an agrarian biblical world, was a sign of abundance. In other words, the mere fact that Gideon had wheat to thresh was a symbol of God's favor expressed to His people, despite the hardship and oppression they were facing.

Gideon's story reveals that even your most mundane duty has a twinkle of the favor of God. For if He removed His blessings completely from you—taking away your home, your family, your work, your possessions—the need for many of your daily tasks would disappear. Don't despise the very things that signify your seat under the umbrella of God's goodness each day.

See Digging Deeper III "The Principle of Abundance and Oppression" for more.

Look back at the list of routine tasks you wrote down earlier. Beside each, write down what they indicate about God's faithfulness and kindness to you.

Gideon threshed because God was kind. Had God chosen to withhold that kindness, Israel would not only have been displaced and browbeaten by the enemy but would also have starved to death from lack of crops. Did Gideon realize that his threshing was a sign of God's favor on him and his people? Probably not. Was he so concerned about the enemy or bored by his task that he didn't realize his actions showed that Yahweh had not abandoned them? Probably so.

What about you? What about me?

I bet our top five ordinary tasks look similar—if not in exact detail, at least in their level of seeming importance. Most of our days are filled with routine duties required for life to continue with any sort of sanity. But if we take the time to look closely, we might discover that God is using these normal activities to prepare us for future tasks, each duty pointing to His blessings in our lives.

End today's lesson by asking the Lord to help you be thankful for those ordinary tasks, to not despise them, and to see how He might be using them to prepare you for the future.

Today my #LessonsFromGideon are:

THE PRINCIPLE OF ABUNDANCE AND OPPRESSION

As you consider Gideon's abundance of wheat, don't miss an important principle. God's people were oppressed by the Midianites. Their dismal plight was a direct consequence of their rebellion. Gideon's tribe, Manasseh, like many other tribes in the nation, had not taken full possession of their land. They fell into idolatry as they mingled with the Canaanites. God was obviously not pleased, yet He supplied His people's needs. The fact that He chose to bless them with wheat to thresh does not imply that He had truly blessed them as a people. They had wheat, but not peace. Grain but not goodwill.

Having an ample wheat supply, therefore, in the midst of this rancid environment tells us something theologically important: both oppression and abundance can coexist in the lives of God's people. God's loyalty does not equal God's approval. In 1 Chronicles 21, for example, David's sin had resulted in dire consequences for Israel. A tormenting plague swept through the land for three days, wiping out 70,000 people. Yet in the midst of this tragedy, the Bible says a guy named Ornan "was threshing wheat" (v. 20). Divine discipline and consequence were running rampant across the hills and valleys of Israel, yet the people were still experiencing the great mercy of the Lord (v. 13). How do we know? Because their threshing floors remained full.

The harvest that God routinely allowed Israel's farmers to retain was not a sign of God's approval; it was a sign of His loyalty. I wonder if Israel ever confused the two. I wonder if we ever confuse them.

Consider and internalize the Principle of Abundance and Oppression:

1. God is still faithful to us even when we are faithless.

2. God's faithfulness does not signify God's approval.

May we never equate His faithfulness to us in times of rebellion with His endorsement or tolerance of our choices. When we are unfaithful to God, He will not excuse or overlook our sin. But because we are His, He will still demonstrate His love and care by remaining faithful to His covenant with us and populating our lives with certain blessings. These gifts are not designed to lull us into spiritual apathy or lighten the weight of our offenses. He intends to woo us, graciously, kindly, lavishly—back into intimate fellowship with Himself.

OVERLOOKING THE OBVIOUS

The angel of the LORD appeared to him and said to him, "The LORD is with you, O valiant warrior."
Judges 6:12

Ordinary.

This week we're learning that the ordinary is often the disguise of the divine. God often comes to us in ways that are unassuming, steadying us as we become aware of His constant, active presence. But because we often lose sight of His glory under a pile of routine activities, we sometimes miss the stunning and powerful messages He comes to give.

From the verse in the margin, record the first part of the declaration the angel made to Gideon.

What might have caused Gideon to doubt this revelation?

The Lord was with him? Really? If there was one thing Gideon felt extremely certain of, it was that God had completely abandoned him and his people. How else could their circumstances have become this disastrous for this long?

According to Judges 6:13, what questions did Gideon ask the angel?

The fact that Gideon had these frank, bold questions is understandable. For the seventh year in a row, Israel had been sitting ducks for Midian's annual hunting trip. Gideon, like anyone else in this scenario, had some questions about how these things could occur if God was as near as this stranger was suggesting.

If you're facing a season of difficulty, write down the questions you've been asking God on the left side of this chart. We'll come back to these thoughts a little later today.

Questions for God	His Answers

There's nothing wrong with a question … unless you've already been given the answer.

GIDEON'S QUESTIONS, GOD'S ANSWERS

Jude, my four-year-old, often asks me the same question over and over again, sometimes within the span of a few minutes.

"Mommy? Mommy? Mommy? Mommy?"

"Can I? Can I? Can I? Can I?"

While continuous questions can be bothersome, the only time I get truly unnerved is when I've already answered them. Doesn't he know by now that my answer isn't going to change—that once I've made up my mind, there's no point in asking again?

Maybe one day he'll figure it out.

Maybe one day … I will too.

GIDEON

Read Judges 6:8-10 in your Bible. Which of the following does verse 10 pinpoint as the source of Israel's problems?
☐ Israel had served idols and disobeyed God.
☐ Israel had been abandoned by God.
☐ Israel was living in the wrong land.

Go back to Gideon's questions you recorded on page 50. Circle the one that Judges 6:10 answers.

In the midst of Israel's long, tumultuous plight, God had sent a nameless prophet to them. This anonymous bearer of divine insight had given the answer as to why terrible things were happening. Instead of needing to search out new information with the angel in verse 13, Gideon needed only to recall what he had heard some time before in verse 10.

Just like my three-year-old.

Shoot … just like me.

Far too often, I spend time asking God about matters He has already explained. In His Word, He has listed His decisions. I should not expect Him to change His mind just because I keep bringing it up. No matter how fervent the prayer or how pious my kneeling position, I cannot get a different answer out of God.

No need to ask Him about some things. He's written down His response in eternal ink. I might as well stop asking … and start reading.

WHY DO YOU ASK?

Instead of answering Gideon's litany of complaints, the angel responded, "Go in this your strength and deliver Israel from the hand of Midian. Have I not sent you?" (Judg. 6:14).

Huh? I asked you a question, buddy. Let's start with an answer for that! But no answer would come to Gideon, for the angel had already moved on to other things. New things. God had already made Himself clear on the previous ones. The revelation of God's nearness and His previously given Word to the people were all Gideon would need for doing what He was being called to do.

Now, I believe God graciously allows us to come to Him with questions that stir our souls when life doesn't make sense. But, Sister, God's Word has already spoken on so many of the topics that you and I are constantly asking questions about. Whether regarding our spiritual destiny or our practical daily experiences, we sometimes need only recall what God has already said to get the answer we are so fervently seeking in prayer.

> The Lord's command to go forward in his strength was a reference to the Spirit's strength with which Yahweh intended to clothe and empower Gideon.

It is wise to seek God for direction as we apply spiritual principles to specific decisions in our lives (as we'll see later in Gideon's story). But sometimes—*sometimes*—prayer and fasting are unnecessary steps in knowing what God is saying. When we feel God is ignoring us, could it be that His perceived silence is intended to point us back to His Word? Take time to see what's already written in Scripture. If God said it then, He still means it now.

> **Choose two of these verses to look up. Record what they say is clearly God's will for people.**
> - Micah 6:8
>
> - 1 Thessalonians 4:3
>
> - 1 Thessalonians 5:18
>
> - Ephesians 6:6
>
> - Matthew 22:37-38

If God said it then, He still means it now.
#LessonsFromGideon

THAT'S THE TRUTH

Gideon somehow experienced a disconnect between what he'd heard before and what he was currently facing. Either he never really gave God credit for all those miracles of deliverance and conquest (as the prophet had reminded Israel in Judges 6:8-10) or he just didn't think God was around anymore and willing to do those same things for him. He heard, "The LORD is with you," but he didn't believe it.

> **While we can't say for certain why Gideon failed to recall God's promises, which option(s) best indicate why we often don't?**
> ☐ We never heard it in the first place.
> ☐ We hear but forget when difficulty arises.
> ☐ We don't seek out God's prerecorded responses to our questions.
> ☐ We don't believe what we read.
> ☐ We don't think it applies to us.
> ☐ We think God might change His mind for us because our circumstances are unique.

Choose one from the list that describes a frame of mind or attitude you've recently exhibited. What causes you to justify this response?

For Group Discussion: On page 36, we considered our tendency to stress our own logic over God's truth. How do you see hints of this in today's portion of Gideon's story? How do we tend to react like Gideon did in this situation?

No matter Gideon's reasons, you and I need to learn a lesson from this event: God's Word is sure, unchanging, and true. This means it doesn't vary or fall prey to our realities, no matter how difficult or even hopeful His statement is. Rather, His Word stands over our circumstances as the declarative reality to which all of our lives—and everything happening within them—must answer and be conformed.

The truth: Yahweh was with Gideon. The truth: He had been and still was their deliverer. The truth: Israel needed only to turn from her wickedness, and she would begin to see this fact clearly. God said it. Now Gideon needed to believe it ... and live according to it.

Prayerfully consider answers God has already given to any of the questions you recorded earlier (page 51). Write your answers on the right side of the chart.

If you can't find biblical responses to your questions or uncertainties, take them to a spiritual leader who can help you find the answers in God's Word and pray with you about them.

God is with you, Sister. Yeah, I'm talking to *you*. God is with you, just like He was with Gideon.

No matter what He's commissioning you to do—to fearlessly parent your children alone, faithfully submit to authority, courageously begin that ministry, boldly walk in moral purity, surrender to the demands of this season—whatever it is, recklessly follow Him. Because if He is with you, then no one and nothing can ever be against you.

Today my #LessonsFromGideon are:

DAY 4
WHO DO YOU THINK YOU ARE?

I looked in the mirror and grimaced at the sight of a dark spot on my lower back. I'd noticed it for the past two evenings while getting ready for bed, and I was officially concerned. I turned my back toward the mirror on my closet door and twisted my head around to take a good look.

What in the world could it be? I didn't know. But after watching it for two days, I knew one thing: I was calling the doctor in the morning.

I decided to mention it to my husband, who turned me around and took a quick peek. "Don't see anything," he said and returned to his book.

Unconvinced he was taking this seriously, I told him to look a second time ... right ... here. Again, he saw nothing. Either God had performed a quick miracle on me, or Jerry was in need of one—for blindness.

At that, I forced him into the bathroom with me, spun my body into the same position under the shaded bathroom lights, and pointed out the bruise I couldn't believe he couldn't see.

Thank goodness, he could finally spot it. He squinted his eyes into tiny slants two inches away from my skin. But after a few seconds, he grabbed my right elbow and tugged me six inches to the right, then smirked and walked back to the bedroom. The spot on my lower back was suddenly, amazingly, completely gone. It had been only a shadow.

A change in perspective changed everything.

SHIFTING SHADOWS

Gideon has had a shadow cast across his life. It has left him feeling deflated, worried, and dispirited. For seven years he has lived with an ominous Midianite silhouette settling itself across his soul, causing an outline of discouragement around him.

So one of the primary goals of the angel at the moment of their meeting was to give the soon-to-be judge a swift tug out of the shadows and into the clarifying light of Yahweh's perspective.

> Fill in the blanks from Judges 6:12 (HCSB):
> "The Lord is with you, _____ _____."

Which of the following were the focus of this portion of the angel's message to Gideon?

☐ what he had been called to do
☐ who he had been called to defeat
☐ who he was
☐ who was with him
☐ who he had been called to lead

"Mighty warrior" in Hebrew is *gibbor chayil,* also translated as "mighty man of valor" in the King James Version. The terminology is the same used to describe David's valiant warriors who had executed courageous exploits on behalf of the king (1 Chron. 11:10-25). This label made sense for David's warriors. They were elite fighters, handpicked to perform special tasks. They were champions. When others wilted under pressure, these men stood their ground, undeterred in support of their new king.

Underline the key words in the paragraph above that describe a *gibbor chayil*.

Considering Gideon's current posture, what would have made the angel's statement ironic and unbelievable?

Gideon didn't have the look of a "mighty man of valor." Cowering silently in the winepress, Gideon felt and looked like anything other than valiant. Nobody would have described this man with our Hebrew term. But Yahweh's view was not bound by Gideon's reality or actions. Gideon may have been under the shadow of Midian, but Yahweh was not. He could see beyond the exterior, calling out of Gideon something that the timid man probably didn't even realize was in him. Gideon wasn't a scared farmer. Not really. That's how he was behaving, but that's not who he was.

Yahweh's perspective of us is often so unbelievable, so foreign to our own belief system and conduct that it can be like a bolt of lightning striking our desensitized souls. It jolts us away from the misplaced shadows of our experience into the truth of God's reality.

The angel had already told Gideon Who was *with him,* but now he wanted to reveal what was *in him.* The angel knew that Gideon wouldn't respond well to the call until his perception of his potential was reformatted. So the angel tugged the would-be hero out of the shadows and into the clear, bright light of Yahweh's love.

Behavior does not
determine identity.
#LessonsFromGideon

Why do you think it is critical for believers to understand their identity before moving forward into their destiny?

If you've ever seen how an incorrect or malformed spiritual identity can hamper someone's spiritual success, describe it in the margin and prepare to share it with your group.

Who you are is more important than what you have been called to do.
#LessonsFromGideon

BELIEVE IT OR NOT

So Gideon was a mighty warrior, huh? Well, apparently he wasn't buying it.

Read Gideon's response to the angel in Judges 6:13. How did Gideon deal with the angel's sentiments about him being a valiant warrior?
☐ He refuted it.
☐ He hesitantly acknowledged it.
☐ He received it, believed it, and walked in it.
☐ He ignored it completely.
☐ He applied it to someone else.

Mark the pair of terms that best describe a disparity you've dealt with between your self-perception and a biblical view of who you are in Christ.

Self-image	God-image	Bible Reference
fearful	courageous	Josh. 1:9, Ps. 138:3
incompetent	capable	2 Cor. 3:5-6
ungifted	equipped	1 Cor. 1:4-8, Heb. 13:20-21
worthless	valuable	1 Pet. 2:9, Matt. 6:26
rejected	accepted	John 15:16
insignificant	special	Zeph. 3:17, Eph. 1:3-6

Have you seen this impact your ability to walk in a way that is pleasing to the Lord? If so, how?

GIDEON

Keep a reminder of God's Word to you in this area of your life. On a 3x5 card, write the pair of words you selected. On the other side, record the Scripture God has given you for this issue. Keep it handy all week.

Record the reasons why you chose the pair(s) of words you did, and then look up the corresponding verse(s) to read and prayerfully consider.

I cannot even begin to tell you how many times I've brushed past God's exclamations of His view of me. Sometimes, instead of acting in a way that is congruent with what He says, I casually dismiss it as something that might be true for others but not for me. Without Him, left to my own reality, I am all of those "fearful, incompetent, insignificant" things in the list. But with Him, my purposes and possibilities completely change.

Gideon was so skeptical of the description God had given him, he didn't even address the whole *gibbor chayil* title in his response. Immersed in the throes of devastation and disillusionment, he discussed another theme entirely. In essence, Gideon overlooked one of the most important portions of this heavenly interaction.

Sometimes, so do we.

Earlier, you selected the option that best describes how Gideon dealt with the angel's sentiments. Go back and circle the option that describes how you most often deal with what God says about you.

Think specifically about the passages you looked up earlier. Is there any part of God's viewpoint of your identity or potential that you have dismissed or disregarded? Why?

What would "receiving it, believing it, and walking in it" look like in your life? What would change about the next twenty-four hours of your life if you believed what God said?

GROUNDWORK

Sometimes we prematurely pursue the mission to which we've been called and forgo the critical groundwork of learning about and walking in our God-given spiritual identity. When life's shadows distort our reality, those distortions can easily become our truth, ripping us away from God's truth and thwarting our purpose.

The assignment for which God is calling us will go unrealized unless we are convinced of the spiritual chops He has given us to accomplish it. His perspective might sound unbelievable and even look completely incorrect based on the way we are acting and feeling. But trusting God and walking in His pronouncement of potential is the foundation of spiritual victory.

A believer without a clear sense of her true spiritual identity is like a police officer with no badge, like a driver with no license. They may have the right equipment, but they don't have the authority to use it.

Gideon was more than the sum of his cowardly parts. He was more than his circumstances. He was a valiant warrior touched by an encounter with God Himself. And you, my friend, are too.

Even if you are hiding in a winepress.

Even if you are running from an enemy.

Even if you are more humiliated now than ever before.

Even if intimidation and fear have been your constant companions.

Today, you're getting tugged out of the shadows. Now, lift up your head and act like it.

Today my #LessonsFromGideon are:

GIDEON'S ASSIGNMENT

First things first. It's an adage quickly spouted and often as quickly ignored, because we don't know what we should prioritize or we don't like what's first in line when we do.

Any doubts that Gideon's visitor was heavenly had vanished from his mind right along with the angel from his sight (Judg. 6:21). He now knew for sure Who he'd been dealing with at his homemade threshing floor. So Gideon, his uncertainties quelled, built an altar (Judg. 6:24), signifying the beginning of his transfer of allegiance away from the false gods of his people.

As this change was beginning to burn hot in Gideon's heart and mind, Yahweh began to spell out Gideon's very first assignment. He was sending him to a mission field a lot closer than Gideon might have suspected.

> **Fill in the blanks from Judges 6:25:**
> Now on the same night the Lord said to him, "Take your father's young bull and a second bull seven years old, and _____ _____ the altar of _____ which belongs to your _____, and cut down the _____ that is beside it."

That the age of the bull Gideon would slay correlated to the number of years Midian had ravaged Israel was no coincidence. This year, the eighth, would be the last—for both.

Gideon had already been told he would "deliver Israel from the power of Midian" (v. 14). But his ministry wouldn't start there. Gideon was to lead a reformation beginning from the place where he'd opened his eyes that morning.

His own house.

HEARTS TOWARD HOME

Gideon's first assignment seemed contrary to what the angel of the Lord had said to him earlier. Delivering his house from an idol wasn't the first logical step toward delivering Israel from Midian. But the former would be a required stepping stone to the latter. Until Israel was rid of her idols and her fidelity to them, external freedom from hardship would be at best temporary and superficial.

So Gideon's work would begin in the circle closest to him and spread outward from there. The journey of fulfilling our divine purpose will almost always follow this same pattern. Take note of the journey of Gideon's calling.

For more study:
Note who responded when Gideon blew his trumpet to rally his countrymen for battle in Judges 6:34–35. See the outward progression of his influence—throughout his tribe, then throughout the nation.

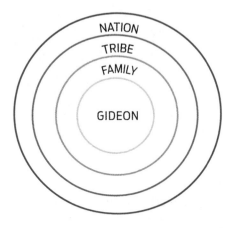

Why do you think Gideon beginning his work in this way was critical to Israel's overarching success?

Record your initials in the smallest of the circles below. In the slightly larger circles, write the next two spheres of influence in your life—the people or environments closest to you.

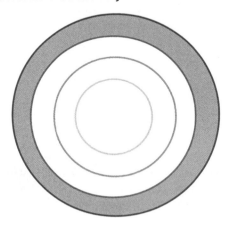

Ministry Spheres of Influence: Start from the inside and work your way out.
#LessonsFromGideon

Prayerfully consider those you just wrote in the chart. What is God asking you to do in relation to them? Why do you think people often avoid these circles?

Choosing to do our primary work in the smaller, less noticeable spheres and devote our best gifts there is often a foreign thought to us. We usually want to jump from the center directly to the perimeter of impact, skipping over the areas most closely connected to us. The result? A life and calling that eventually implode, caving in upon their shoddy, unstable structure.

God had strategically set Gideon in this family, in this tribe, and in this valley for a reason. He fully intended to call and equip Gideon to affect his closest relationships before moving on to something and someone else.

The priority and preeminence of serving those in the sphere closest to us is seen throughout Scripture. When Abraham was chosen by God to be the father of Israel, he was given instructions for what his first tasks should be.

> **Turn to Genesis 18:19. In your own words, what did God tell Abraham to concentrate on prior to experiencing the fulfillment of His promises?**

Centuries later, as Jesus' disciples were ushered into the age of the church, God gave them a unique power to function on His behalf, and then clearly outlined the course their ministry was to follow.

"But you will receive power when the Holy Spirit has come upon you; and you shall be My witnesses both in Jerusalem, and in all Judea and Samaria, and even to the remotest part of the earth."
Acts 1:8

> **From Acts 1:8 in the margin, underline the three spheres of influence mentioned, and then record them in order below:**
>
> 1.
>
> 2.
>
> 3.

The disciples were in Jerusalem when they received these instructions from Jesus. They were to focus on the ministry to be done where they were standing even as they began moving outward on mission. Start inward, move outward.

First things first. Both for Gideon and for us.

IT'S HARDER AT HOME

Gideon had been reared in an idol-worshipping family. His own father was the keeper of the Baal altar in their town of Ophrah.

> ## Answer the following questions, using Judges 6:27 as a guide:
>
> 1. Did Gideon do what God asked him to?
>
> 2. How did he do it?
>
> 3. Why did he do it this way?
>
> 4. What do you think caused him to feel this way?

A Baal altar was found at Megiddo that measured some twenty-six feet across and four and a half feet high. Made of many stones, cemented together by mud, such an altar would constitute an immense task to destroy and carry away.[3]

Often, like in Gideon's case, our smaller spheres of influence are not easier to contend with just because they are smaller. On the contrary, some of the most difficult and intimidating opportunities to walk in God's calling come when we are staring in the faces of those who know us best and whom we love the most.

Consider how Gideon must have felt tearing down what his father had spent his lifetime building, teaching, and defending. With each stone that he and his servants dismantled, another layer of the ideology that had overrun his family came unglued. This overnight idol-demolishing wasn't affecting some random town and family he would never see again. This was a task he'd feel, see, and endure the consequences of every day from that point on.

- When the Christian daughter chooses to evangelize her non-Christian parents …
- When the godly wife chooses to set an example for her unsaved spouse …
- When the teenager seeks to impact his pagan school environment …
- When the coworker tries to influence her friends on the job …

The stakes are often much higher when the mission field is so personal.

I've darkened the outlying circle in the earlier diagram, because what lies ahead in your journey is not nearly as critical as where you are right now. Wherever you are now is where you are meant to serve now. These innermost circles are often the ones that offer the least amount of recognition. This is why so many people try to circumvent them. And yet your greatest impact will be done here—in the ordinary rhythms of your daily living.

What are the two hardest things you'd likely face in serving those in the first two circles of your diagram?

Following God wholeheartedly within these up-close loops of faith will often cause you an internal uneasiness and daily faithfulness that cannot be escaped just because it's 5 p.m. and the workday is over. It's easier to stand on a platform and teach people we may never see again than to walk with our own children, friends, and loved ones in accountability and discipleship. But these spheres encompass the heart of true ministry.

Begin to clarify who the people in your primary sphere of influence should be. Refuse to search for significance in another place if you've bypassed any near and necessary steps in the journey God has for you.

Pray for a courageous faith and holy boldness to start where you are. He'll give it to you.

In the week ahead, we'll see Gideon's trust stretched to the max. For now, take a moment to soak in what God has taught you so far. How have you been challenged? How have you been encouraged? Journal your thoughts and spend some time talking to God as you close this week of our study.

Today my #LessonsFromGideon are:

Session 3
VIEWER GUIDE

They have given Gideon a new name: Jerubbaal means the _____ _____ .

You are not the _____ _____ you used to be.

> Philippians 1:6

Challenge: keep a _____ of the _____ God has been doing.

> Judges 7:1

Harod means to _____, _____.

_____ matters.

_____ is everything.

How you start at the _____ has every bearing on how it's going to _____ in the _____.

Where you choose to _____ determines the _____ _____ from which you take in the enemy's attacks on your life.

> Judges 7:2

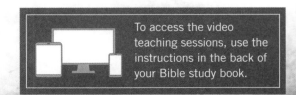

To access the video teaching sessions, use the instructions in the back of your Bible study book.

A BRAND-NEW IDENTITY

You have _____ _____ for Me to give Midian into your hand.

1. You are not the _____ _____ you used to be.

2. You have no business _____ where you used to go.

3. You don't _____ everything you thought you would _____.

    2 Corinthians 12:9

NOTE: *Saul and his army camped at Mt. Gilboa (1 Sam. 28:4) by "the spring which is in Jezreel" (1 Sam. 29:1). According to *The Anchor Bible Dictionary,* this spring would have been the same as the one Gideon and his men used.

(From Logos Bible Software ed. 5, Bellingham, WA. "Elika" from *The Anchor Yale Bible Dictionary.*)

week three

THE KEY TO OUR STRENGTH

I've got a holy sense of anticipation about this week. My spiritual wheels are whirring in excitement over what God will share with us as we jump into this very important section of Gideon's story. If there's a place where each of us can relate to this farmer-turned-warrior, this is it.

We all know how it feels to be ...

Scared.

Outnumbered.

Intimidated.

Exhausted.

And so did Gideon.

Whether they involve the new company that just hired you, the family that needs you, or the ministry that's stretching you, your circumstances can hang like a dead weight across your shoulders. You can feel ill-equipped to handle all the exhausting demands. That pervasive sense of inadequacy—the one that hits you in waves when everything seems completely beyond your capacity—can end up totally paralyzing you.

Gideon almost surely felt the same pressure.

GIDEON

Then Jerubbaal (that is, Gideon) and all the people who were with him, rose early and camped beside the spring of Harod; and the camp of Midian was on the north side of them by the hill of Moreh in the valley.

Judges 7:1

Turn to the Geography of Gideon map on the inside back cover and mark the spring where Gideon's army camped. Draw an arrow to where Midian camped.

Consider Israel's perspective of Midian as described in Judges 7:1. How might this view have affected Israel's morale?

Remember, a main premise in this study is that our weaknesses are the conduits through which we experience God's strength. Weakness is a key, and like most keys, it's designed to open something. God designed your key specifically to fit the lock He has in mind for you. He uses your weaknesses, the areas and places where you feel the least strong, to open a divine door. Without this key, we would rarely experience God's strength.

He didn't pass you over on the manufacturing line when handing out specific gifts or traits. On the contrary, He specifically and uniquely fitted your keys to open divine doors. So today, we're going to talk about how to connect the two: your weakness and God's strength. Gideon was about to get an unforgettable lesson on the subject. So will we.

Complete this statement: "My _____ is the key to unlocking God's _____."

Your confidence (or the lack thereof) will always find its roots in how you handle your key. Your weakness will stay magnified and unused as long as you're focused on it instead of the strength of God it's meant to unleash.

Do you tend to focus on your weaknesses? Yes/No If so, what effect does this have on your

- emotions?

- self-image?

- confidence?

- ability to move forward?

Gideon was an underdog. No matter how impactful his encounters with Yahweh had been, the 32,000 ragtag soldiers he had scrounged together were still no match for a Midianite army of 135,000 (Judg. 8:10) camped in the valley with their impressive caravan of camels. He was completely outnumbered. As long as he focused on the disparity between the forces, his confidence was sure to wane.

Overwhelming situations like these are often God's way of doing business. The Bible is filled with stories of people who got to see their weakness parlayed into a demonstration of Yahweh's strength. Let's look at two of the most impactful and familiar in Scripture.

TOO MANY MOUTHS TO FEED

First, turn to Luke 9:12-17 and answer the following:

What was the problem?

What did the disciples have to fix the problem?

What did Jesus say was the solution?

What two solutions did they propose (vv. 12-13)?

Faced with 15,000 or more hungry people (including the women and children), the disciples decided the best way to achieve success was to send them all away. Problem solved. But Jesus wouldn't allow that, so they proposed a plan B: they would go into the city themselves, hoping the neighboring town would harbor their solution.

Bad idea again.

They, like Gideon, felt outnumbered and beyond their abilities for the same reason: *they were looking at the wrong thing.* Their eyes lingered on their scarce resources and their looming problem—instead of concentrating on the fact that Jesus was with them. Their misplaced focus caused them to feel illegitimately insecure.

I got a visual of this yesterday when my son was running in fear of a playful, energetic dog twice his size. His anxiety faded once he was safely in my arms because his attention had shifted away from the scary dog to the security he found with me. A change in focus changes everything. Consider the two solutions the disciples sought for their situation.

This battle was the first time camels were used in warfare, and this gave the Midianites a staggering advantage over the Israelites. Camels could "sprint up to forty miles per hour, maintain twenty-five miles per hour for an hour, and cover one hundred miles in a day."[1]

How do you usually deal with a situation when you feel outmatched?

☐ I try to send the problem away.

☐ I try to get myself away from the problem.

Explain your answer.

How does a focus on your weaknesses promote the selection you made in the exercise above?

5 + 2 = More than enough
#LessonsFromGideon

I believe the lesson of this remarkable Bible story is not so much about hungry people being fed, but about doubting disciples being reminded of God's available resources. Sending the multitude away would not only have kept the crowd from experiencing a miracle, it would have kept the disciples from being used by Jesus to perform one. The lesson He wanted to teach them was clear: Don't concentrate on the disparity between the problem and your resources. Look to Me, and watch five loaves plus two fish equal more than enough.

The five loaves and two fish were the key that Jesus put in their hands to unlock the door of God's strength. Instead of running from their weaknesses or discounting them, they had been called to use them.

ONE GIGANTIC PROBLEM

When all the men of Israel saw the man, they fled from him and were greatly afraid. The men of Israel said, "Have you seen this man who is coming up?"
1 Samuel 17:24-25

I shy away from been-there-done-that Bible passages for fear that a woman steeped in Bible study, like yourself, might let out a sigh of boredom. But I want you to lay fresh eyes on 1 Samuel 17:24-25 from the familiar story of David and Goliath. I've printed it in the margin for you.

Underline what the Israelite men were looking at.
Circle the emotion this sight inspired in them.

You can almost hear the nervous fear in their voices, asking young David if he'd seen what they were all up against. Oh, yes, David had seen him. But unlike his fellow countrymen, his focus was on something else.

Goliath, the great champion from Gath, had said: "I defy the ranks of Israel this day" (1 Sam. 17:10).

And guess what? David heard Goliath's words (v. 23).

Israel was watching, but David was listening. This small but important difference created a variation in their responses. Sure, David could see the nine-foot, nine-inch giant. (How could he not?) But what he heard made a holy indignation rise up within him, causing him to turn his true focus toward the One who was being blasphemed. It bristled against the fiber of his belief and trust in God.

So while all Israel was paralyzed by what they saw, David was galvanized to action by what he heard. So, He looked to Yahweh, gathered up five little stones and conquered a giant.

David learned the same lesson the disciples did: shift your focus from the key itself to the door God can unlock with it. Use what you have—no matter how weak—and God will take care of the rest.

> For Group Discussion: What would redirecting your focus look like in practical terms? Discuss some strategic things believers can do to redirect their attention off themselves and onto the Lord.

Gideon had 32,000 men. His opponent had four times more. No doubt he was more focused on his deficiency than his Deliverer. God's solution? To put Gideon in a position where he'd have no choice but to refocus his attention. That's what we'll focus on tomorrow.

For now, carefully consider where your focus is. On the hungry multitudes? On the smack-talking giant? On the Midianites? On the enemy? On your problems? On your lack? The key is in knowing where to look. And knowing that even in your weakness, His strength is always ... enough!

Today my #LessonsFromGideon are:

LESS IS MORE

I enjoy jogging ... but I'm not a serious runner. I like to think I am, but I'm reminded I'm not by people on the road who actually are. They are swift, lean, and don't stop to walk (like I do) when they reach an incline. Unlike me, they don't wear a huge gray sweatshirt or long, heavy sweatpants when it's a little chilly outside. The serious runners have on light shoes, ankle socks, running shorts, and a thin T-shirt. If they're sporting any extra attire, it's only the sweatband to catch their perfect beads of sweat or the iPod attached to their chiseled arms.

Yup, serious runners aren't bogged down with too much weight or too many gadgets. They know the secret to short-term success and long-term endurance is to take along as little as possible.

God wanted Gideon's 32,000-man army shaved down. His plan for short-term success and long-term endurance for the nation couldn't be achieved if they carried any excess into battle. That's because His purpose didn't stop and start with a simple victory in this one battle. That might have been Gideon's goal, but it wasn't Yahweh's. God was after something much more intimate and personal.

> The LORD said to Gideon, "You have too many people for Me to hand the Midianites over to you, or else Israel might brag: 'I did it myself.'"
> Judges 7:2

In Judges 7:2, what key words or phrases make clear God's intention for further whittling down this army?

When have any of the words or phrases been true of you? Have you credited yourself, or someone else, with something God did? What do you think caused your oversight? Plan to discuss this with your group.

FORGET ME NOT

> Pride forgets. Humility remembers.
> #LessonsFromGideon

Spiritual amnesia was a regular problem for Israel. They easily forgot Who accomplished good things on their behalf. Even after their divinely orchestrated rescue mission from Egypt, they quickly forgot the kindness and mercy of Yahweh. Thus Moses spent the greater part of the Book of Deuteronomy reminding them of all the things God had done on their behalf. Pride forgets. Humility remembers.

As Gideon and the 32,000 set out for battle, God knew something about His people then that He knows about His people now: when we are even reasonably positioned to excel in a task, we tend to take the credit that rightfully belongs to Him. As long as we can even remotely explain it by numbers, smarts, experience, or good genes, we will try to own what is His. Then we settle further into a dismal pride that wears away our spiritual fiber. We'll talk about this more in-depth, but first look up Judges 8:22.

After the battle, who did the Israelites give credit to and what did they want to do as a result?

How have you seen misdirected credit lead to misplaced trust or unhealthy desires for you or someone else?

Building off Psalm 103:2, what benefits of God's goodness have you experienced lately that you may have given yourself or someone else credit for?

Be careful that your heart doesn't become proud and you forget the LORD your God who brought you out from the land of Egypt, out of the place of slavery. Deuteronomy 8:14, HCSB

Bless the LORD, O my soul, and forget none of His benefits. Psalm 103:2

I think I should give you a heads-up now: this story does not end well. Neither Gideon nor God's people chose wisely at the end of these chapters. As pride crept in, Gideon began to arrogantly take matters into his own hands, and the nation again returned to idolatry.

As I studied, I'll admit I was so frustrated at this, I wanted to reach back and give the Israelites a good slap. But one thing always stopped me: I've been one of those people too! Gideon's army was about to be shaved down for the same reason the Lord often allows us to be shorthanded. He knew the greater the odds in battle, the more likely Israel would have been, and the more likely we are, to lean toward humility.

So the 32,000 would become 300. The odds increased from 4:1 to an astronomical, unthinkable 450:1. Thus God minimized pride's chances of taking credit for a victory.

OPEN THE DOOR

Remember what we studied yesterday? Our weakness is the key God uses to unlock the door, but even an unlocked door must still be opened. Humility is the knob we grasp that causes the door of God's power to

Weakness unlocks the door. Humility opens it.
#LessonsFromGideon

Humility is not thinking unkindly about yourself. It's being willing to set yourself aside for a more important purpose.

Give me neither poverty nor riches! Give me just enough to satisfy my needs. For if I grow rich, I may deny you and say, "Who is the Lord?"
Proverbs 30:8-9, NLT

be opened wide in our lives. While pride, arrogance, and self-reliance incur God's opposition and shut the door of His favor, humility fosters a dependence upon Him, unleashing His power in our lives.

If anything was going to be the downfall of these people, it wouldn't be Midian; it would be Israel's pride. So God purposefully, lovingly stripped down Gideon's army to the bare bones, leaving them no choice but to rely on Yahweh for victory.

Look at the arrows below. When God allows our self-reliance and strength to go down in an area, our level of humility and God-dependence almost always goes up. When we feel equipped and competent, our humility tends to plummet into an abyss of pride that hinders God's work in our lives.

This doesn't mean we shouldn't celebrate our gifts and talents, but it does mean we should be more vigilant about guarding our humility when we're using those gifts. On the other hand, we need not see our weaknesses as repulsive, but as helpful in developing our continued dependence on God.

Personalize these arrows. In the space provided, write a key word that reminds you of an area that's causing an increase of humility in your life. In the second set, record a key word that describes an area that could be contributing to an increase of pride.

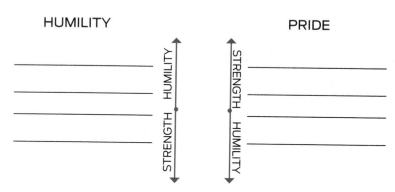

What are some practical strategies you can put in place for fostering and maintaining humility?

BEFORE A FALL

Many of Gideon's unwise choices in later years were directly connected to the underhanded enemy of pride. So we do well to do business with God on this issue right away, being careful to cling ferociously to humility.

Which, if any, of these consequences have been most apparent in your life? In what way?

Connect each of the following passages with the consequences of pride. I've done one for you.

_F_ Pride misleads you.	A. I will break down your strong pride. I will make your sky like iron and your land like bronze (Lev. 26:19).
___ Pride hinders you from speaking the truth.	B. In all his scheming, the wicked arrogantly thinks: "There is no accountability, since God does not exist" (Ps. 10:4)
___ Pride incurs the judgment of God	C. Let lying lips be quieted; they speak arrogantly against the righteous with pride and contempt (Ps. 31:18).
___ Pride stirs dissension and keeps you from hearing and heeding good advice.	D. Arrogance leads to nothing but strife, but wisdom is gained by those who take advice (Prov. 13:10).
___ Pride creates a spirit of autonomy and keeps you from seeking God.	E. My adversaries trample me all day, for many arrogantly fight against me (Ps. 56:2).
___ Pride causes you to make unfair judgments and attack others.	F. Your presumptuous heart has deceived you (Obad. 3).

Pride is the hidden cause behind destroyed relationships, stunted spiritual growth, and thwarted emotional healing. Many of life's external difficulties find their roots in this internal reality. So how about we draw a line in the sand of our hearts and evict this horrendous tenant once and for all?

Many of life's external difficulties find their roots in the internal reality of pride.
#LessonsFromGideon

Thank the Lord for the gift of weakness that continues to cultivate a state of humility in your life.

Today my #LessonsFromGideon are:

DOUBLE TROUBLE

As we watch God winnow Gideon's troops today, I want to be clear that having ample resources to fight and succeed is not a bad thing. I've known folks who are exceptionally gifted in a particular area, profoundly financially secure, or even blessed with an unfair amount of good looks, yet who have maintained a keen sense of humility. Nothing is wrong with having strengths. In fact, you already have them ... and should celebrate them. It should only concern you when the extra—the "more"—begins to water down the potency of what should matter most in your life and character.

"Be on guard, so that your hearts will not be weighted down."
Luke 21:34

Like when abundant gifting starts chipping away at your humility. Or when more money dilutes your childlike trust in God. Or when a busier schedule pulls you constantly away from your family. Sometimes more isn't better, and Gideon was about to find out why it wasn't best for him. God knew (as only God knows) that an army this size had the potential to cause damage not only to the enemy but, oddly, to the army itself.

Today, we'll look at the way God chose to whittle down the army. His methods give us hints as to what kind of havoc too many Israelite soldiers could ultimately have done to Israel ... and what an overloaded arsenal of resources can also do to us.

STRENGTH IN NUMBERS?

Military tacticians agree that positive morale is one of the most critical weapons in a soldier's arsenal, and the fastest way for a soldier's optimism to wane is to be in close proximity with another soldier who is panic-stricken. Fear and insecurity can spread like wildfire in a group, weaving a taut fabric of terror that will encumber success.

"Now therefore come, proclaim in the hearing of the people, saying, 'Whoever is afraid and trembling, let him return and depart from Mount Gilead.'" So 22,000 people returned, but 10,000 remained.
Judges 7:3

> Underline the words in Judges 7:3 that pinpoint the kinds of soldiers Gideon was to send home. Circle the number of people who fit this description.

Gideon's heart must have failed as more than two-thirds of his army began to drift away from his battalion—probably one by one at first, then in huge, swarming groups as it became easier and more anonymous to join the mass exodus. I can only imagine how he must have longingly looked at what he was losing, thinking that any chance of victory was following the muddy footprints of those headed home.

Yet this strategy of God's was not a game. He had a tactical reason for this mode of operation—one with an ancient context.

> The law for God's people concerning battle was spelled out in Deuteronomy 20:8. Read the verse and then answer the following questions:
>
> 1. Who were the officers to single out?
>
> 2. What were those who fit in this category to do?
>
> 3. Why?

To maintain a sense of encouragement and optimism, God told the Hebrews to send home anyone fearful. Sure, keeping them around provided a perceived strength in numbers, but it also meant they'd have more difficulty rallying to courageous action. Unhindered fear would have become a more powerful weapon against Israel than the swords in the hands of their enemies.

Let me tell you, the Lord had to do some hard training to get me to see the application of this principle in my life. It seemed strange that having more of something could make me more fearful or insecure. But the lesson became clear when I noticed a neighbor outside in his driveway every evening after work, meticulously and painstakingly cleaning every speck of dirt off his brand new car. Doesn't having a nicer car increase your anxiety about getting it nicked or dirty? Doesn't having more clients make you fearful of meeting all their needs? Can having more clothes and accessories be an indication that you're afraid you might not be well-perceived without them? Is 32,000 always better than 300? Maybe not.

> Is any one thing or relationship contributing to a sense of insecurity or fear in you? If you're not sure, prayerfully ask the Lord to reveal what He wants to show you in this regard.

> Has your confidence in your ability and in God been enhanced as you've moved forward with less? How?

"Fear not" is a biblical declaration that rings from one end of Scripture to the other. In fact, it's recorded more than 300 times, including:

- to Abraham, struggling to believe God's promises (Gen. 26:24)
- to Joseph's brothers, owning their past deeds (Gen. 50:19)
- to Joshua, trying to fill Moses' leadership shoes (Josh. 8:1)
- to Ruth, helpless and needy at the feet of Boaz (Ruth 3:11)
- to Daniel, facedown at a terrifying, riverside vision (Dan. 10:12)
- to Paul, steadying himself on a sinking ship (Acts 27:24)

The way into their blessing, discovery, deliverance, or victory could not be accompanied by fear. Neither could Gideon's. Neither can yours. The Lord is committed to removing anything from your life that might promote the very thing that will hinder your progress.

STAYING ALERT

Judges 7:5-6 gives the second test for whittling down Gideon's troops. Take a look at these verses in the margin.

> **Mark the two positions Gideon was to look for as the men quenched their thirst at the river.**

So he brought the people down to the water. And the LORD said to Gideon, "You shall separate everyone who laps the water with his tongue as a dog laps, as well as everyone who kneels to drink." Now the number of those who lapped, putting their hand to their mouth, was 300 men; but all the rest of the people kneeled to drink water.
Judges 7:5-6

Without regard for the pending war, 9,700 of the remaining 10,000 men caved to the desires of their body, completely diverting their eyes from the menacing surroundings and bending down to the refreshing pool at their feet. Only 300 of them, though equally thirsty, kept their bearings. Their eyes darted away from the enemy-infested hillside only long enough to scoop water into their hands and up to their watchful, scanning faces. Their thirst needed to be quenched—and it was—but not at the expense of their alertness and readiness for war.

While this filtering method is not as clear as the previous one, and while God never specifies the reasoning, it appears their alertness was being tested. Ultimately, God made a divine selection of the 300.

Gideon needed soldiers who were fully devoted and would not be distracted from their primary purpose by the desires of their flesh. Over time, unfocused soldiers might have begun to contaminate the others, dissuading them from their purpose and discouraging their single-mindedness.

My friend Ella has seen her "32,000" depleted recently. Last year, her life was filled to capacity with a flourishing job, a steady loving relationship, a group of girls she discipled, and three roommates who shared a house and a thriving friendship. In the past six months, however, her responsibilities at work shifted, her year-long relationship ended, she completed her position as leader of the discipleship group, and two of her roommates moved away.

These changes left her feeling unsettled and unsure about her future. But she's crystal clear on one thing: her full life had been distracting her from her primary purposes and divine calling. With the excess trimmed away, she can see clearly the personal and physical needs she had been leaving unattended. The reduction process has been painful, but now she is more alert and fully present to participate in God's work in her life.

> Think again about anything the Lord might be stripping from your life. In what ways, if any, have these things dampened your spiritual sensitivity, distracted you from God's purposes, or heightened your fleshly desires and tendencies?

> In all honesty, would you prefer to keep what God is asking you to release or would you rather have the sharpness and clarity that letting it go would allow you to have? Explain your answer.

Be dressed in readiness, and keep your lamps lit.
Luke 12:35

You may not be particularly happy with the 300 you've been left with. I completely understand that, trust me. But according to 2 Corinthians 12:9, "Power is perfected in weakness." The 300 is our secret weapon. It's a showground for God's strength. It's not "more," but it is better because it's what God will use to bring victory into our lives.

Today my #LessonsFromGideon are:

LETTING GO

I live in Texas, where things are lauded for how large they are. We celebrate with enthusiasm everything from T-bone steaks to high, sprayed hair. So the "less is more" philosophy of God's kingdom has been a difficult philosophy for me to get rooted into my Dallas born-and-bred psyche.

> **How do you see the "bigger is better" mentality emphasized in your spheres of influence? How has this pressure affected you? Your family?**

LETTING GO

> The LORD said to Gideon, "I will deliver you with the 300 men ... so let all the other people go."
> Judges 7:7

Gideon's 300 men were outmatched so severely that victory over Midian not only seemed impossible but unthinkable. Imagine how stunned he must have been to hear Yahweh's emphatic declaration of victory spoken loudly over his scanty group: "I will deliver you with the 300."

This tiny statement tucked within the Old Testament has become a powerful declaration of hope and victory for me personally, and within it lies seminal insight for Gideon and for us: the other 31,700 would have hindered the victory assigned to the 300. Keeping more would have actually been to Gideon's detriment.

My friend Chelsea knows about this. She has often told me that while she's blessed with many rich friendships in this season of her life, it has not always been this way. In fact, I was her first real, close girl-friend. And we didn't connect until she was nearly forty years old.

> Bigger doesn't always mean better.
> #LessonsFromGideon

Chelsea was a shy child who constructed many emotional walls to protect her fragile heart from her father's critical, volatile personality. She learned from childhood how to walk on eggshells, shelve her real feelings, and mask her authentic self for the sake of keeping peace and stability. Her internal defense mechanisms became her security blanket. But while they have offered her the comfort of familiarity and perceived emotional safety, they have also cost her fulfilling relationships with those she loves the most.

As the Lord has shown her the disservice these emotional defenses have caused, He has gently but sternly begun to strip them away and expose the tender places she's kept in hiding for so long. Hers has been a difficult and scary journey—letting people in, saying what she really feels, being herself—but she realizes now that her 32,000 wasn't serving her well. Her victory has come from living with less. With her 300.

If you had to pinpoint an area of your life to label "the 300"—an area where you feel depleted or deficient—what category(s) would it fall into?

☐ time   ☐ emotional stability
☐ finances   ☐ talents/gifts
☐ energy   ☐ opportunity
☐ passion   ☐ other
☐ relationships

Grab your Bible and turn to Judges 7:9-11. How confident was Gideon in God's announcement of victory? What leads you to this conclusion?

Which best describes your insecurities when you consider the meager 300 God has given you for accomplishing your journey? How do you feel?

☐ fearful   ☐ doubtful
☐ accepting   ☐ bereft/alone
☐ confident   ☐ anxious
☐ other

What specifically causes you to feel that way?

Can you pinpoint any ways your feelings coincide or conflict with the truth of God?

As his troops dwindled, Gideon must have felt exactly like Chelsea: exposed, vulnerable, and susceptible to danger. But even though Gideon felt insecure, he needed only to recall the divine declaration of triumph God had just given. They would have victory ... because God said so.

In response to God's declaration of victory, what does He instruct Gideon to do in Judges 7:7?

Why do you think Gideon needed to be told this? What might have been his inclination otherwise?

What is your normal response when faced with letting go?

Letting go is hard to do. If Gideon had started with 300 soldiers, he possibly might have had an easier time accepting the notion of going into battle with those. But his trumpet call had originally summoned 32,000. He had seen the hillsides covered with thousands of his countrymen willing to fight. The view now, however, was massively different. The contrast would have been a startling and humbling sight—one that could have scared him into holding onto what God was asking him to release.

Gratefully, Gideon let them go. Will you?

How do any of the thoughts shared in the previous paragraph relate to your experience and difficulty in letting go?

GOING. GOING. GONE.

Oh, how I wish I were with you right now, sitting in your Bible study group, joining you in deep, rich conversation over this lesson today. If I were, I'd tell you that my 300 is in the area of time. Twenty-four hours is never enough for me. It seems that the more time I need, the less I actually have.

Before having children, I felt like I had all the hours in the world to study, write, and plan for ministry. Now, as my children mature, my hours seem to be squeezed. I'm doing what I love, spending time with them, but I've been left with scattered and shortened time slots to fit in ministry. Gideon's story is teaching me that the secret to experiencing victory is not in frantically trying to hang on to my precious hours, but in surrendering them to His purposes. If I will choose to operate in obedient trust, He will multiply my efforts no matter what I'm doing.

I've now noticed that the lessening of my available hours to concentrate solely on ministry tasks has helped decrease some of my sense of fear and worry. Somehow, having more time to think about a looming project or an upcoming conference actually made me feel more daunted by it. Doing more with less has encouraged me to use my time more wisely and to trust Him more fully to multiply my efforts within the time I do have. This new paradigm has enabled me to live more wholly in the moment, to appreciate what God has placed before me, and to find my confidence not in what I've done but in what He's done and is doing.

The secret is not in retaining but in releasing.

> Don't try to retain what God is asking you to release.
> #LessonsFromGideon

Prayerfully consider your personal circumstances in light of the highlighted portions of the Scripture below. In the margin, write observations and personal applications the Holy Spirit uses to speak to you.

Then the LORD said to Elijah, "Go and live in the village of Zarephath, near the city of Sidon. I have instructed a widow there to feed you." So he went to Zarephath. As he arrived at the gates of the village, he saw a widow gathering sticks, and he asked her, "Would you please bring me a little water in a cup?" As she was going to get it, he called to her, "Bring me a bite of bread, too." But she said, "I swear by the LORD your God that I don't have a single piece of bread in the house. And I have only a handful of flour left in the jar and a little cooking oil in the bottom of the jug. I was just gathering a few sticks to cook this last meal, and then my son and I will die." But Elijah said to her, "Don't be afraid! Go ahead and do just what you've said, but make a little bread for me first. Then use what's left to prepare a meal for yourself and your son. For this is what the LORD, the God of Israel, says: There will always be flour and olive oil left in your containers until the time when the Lord sends rain and the crops grow again!" So she did as Elijah said, and she and Elijah and her family continued to eat for many days. There was always enough flour and olive oil left in the containers, just as the LORD had promised through Elijah (1 Kings 17:8-16, NLT).

This woman's future security was discovered in letting go of what she had at her disposal, even though doing so didn't seem reasonable or logical. Had she held onto the oil in an effort to take care of herself, her stock would have been depleted after her next meal. In other words, it would have depleted anyway. But in releasing what the Lord asked of her (when He asked it), she experienced a multiplying miracle.

What is the Lord asking you to release to Him—time, money, security, stability, relationships? Maybe it's hard to see it go because it's been so plentiful in your life and has brought you so much comfort. Understandable.

But take a deep breath ... and then let it go anyway.

I assure you, you'll be better off with God's 300 than your 32,000 every single time.

Today my #LessonsFromGideon are:

DAY 5
THE UNSEEN SUPPLY

Two pennies. That's all my son had when his pudgy, little hands emerged from his pants pockets. He was discouraged. The toy he wanted at the dollar store would require much more than that. He needed ninety-eight more cents, plus tax, to be able to take his new prize home.

I saw his disappointment and my heart broke—not because he didn't have enough, but because he did, and he just didn't know it.

This week, we've watched Gideon's slim hopes of victory dwindle from a tenuous 32,000 soldiers to a much leaner, impossibly outnumbered band of 300. Why did Gideon need only this handful of men to be victorious in battle? Why did Jesus' disciples need only five loaves and two fish to feed 15,000 people? Why did David need only five small stones pulled from a dry riverbed to slay a nearly ten-foot giant?

I found the answer while in aisle B of the Dollar Store, looking at my little boy with those two little pennies in his hand.

WHEN GOD GETS DRESSED

Sister, you have enough. Hear me loud and clear: YOU HAVE ENOUGH. As did my son while standing there in a hopeless pool of despair. Jude had enough for his current need not because of what was at his disposal, but because of what was at mine. No, he didn't have nearly enough money in his own pocket to secure that toy. But I did. Since I'm his mother, not only were my resources available to him, but I was ready and waiting to share them. Just because they were unseen didn't mean they weren't there. He had full access to my resources because of our relationship.

> **Read Judges 6:14 and 34a. Record any connection you would draw between these two passages.**

Your resources are in your relationship.
#LessonsFromGideon

In Judges 6:14, Gideon seems to be commanded to deliver the people based on his own strength and ability. But we've already seen that Gideon was not strong and confident. He was steeped in fear and noted for his insecurity. Yet a sturdy theological bridge connects verses 14 and 34.

GIDEON

The phrase "The Spirit of the LORD came upon" appears six times in reference to the judges (3:10; 6:34; 11:29; 14:6; 14:19; 15:14). In most instances the phrase means "to fall upon mightily." In Gideon's case it meant "to embody."

Until the latter verse, Gideon was just a weak farmhand with no sense of warrior in him, but in verse 34 the English Standard Version describes the moment with the word *clothed*. The Hebrew word *to clothe* (*labash*) normally "referred to the every day act of putting on a garment" and was rarely used in the context of God's Spirit as in this passage.[2]

Get the picture: God's Spirit put on Gideon like a suit of clothes. His flesh became the wardrobe God put on to serve His own purposes. Gideon was now an instrument of obedience—a vessel for God's engine. His actions had become an expression of God's leadership. Now that's power!

When people looked at Gideon, they might still see the same old guy, but he would be anything but. Gideon's previous weaknesses had literally become exchanged with the strength of God. He was filled with the power and the very person of God Himself. He was now ready to be a tool operating according to Yahweh's will.

Indulge me for a moment, OK? I wish there were a more dignified way to illustrate this concept to you, but this simple exercise, while a bit trite, will give you a clear visual of God's Spirit at work in you. Ready?

> **Look at the clothes you have on. Follow the instructions and then answer the question.**
>
> **Move your arm. What does your sleeve do? Why?**
>
> **Move your leg. What does your pant leg do? Why?**
>
> **Considering this simple exercise, describe the believer's relationship with the Spirit of God.**

Gideon's meager army may have seemed insufficient. Paltry even. But the 300 were not all he had at his disposal. The unseen authority of God's own Spirit was within Gideon now, filling him with the most lavish resource of all—divine power. Gideon could enjoy complete confidence no matter how miniscule he deemed his army because he was only a vessel now, a chamber for God. He was merely God's outfit, put on for this special occasion. Knowing this fact changed everything for Gideon ... and it still does for us today.

The Greek equivalent of the Hebrew word *labash* (to clothe) is ***endynamoō*** and appears in the New Testament numerous times. Choose two of the following references and try to determine the word or phrase you think would coincide with the strength of God's Spirit being clothed with Gideon.

Romans 4:20

Philippians 4:13

1 Timothy 1:12

2 Timothy 2:1

2 Timothy 4:17

Hebrews 11:34

For Group Discussion: What conclusions do you draw from the similarities and differences between Ephesians 6:10-17 and Gideon's situation?

Ephesians 6:10-17 gives instructions for how the believer should prepare for spiritual warfare. The Greek word we've been studying (*endynamoō*) is found in verse 10. This tells us that our preparation to wage war against our enemy is not too dissimilar from how Gideon was being prepared to wage war against his.

POWER PLUS

In the very first day of our study this week, you considered the familiar story from Luke 9 of the feeding of the 5,000. A less frequently mentioned part of that situation carries considerable significance as we ponder our own unseen supply.

Read Luke 9:1-2 in the margin. Record as many details as you can about what happened to the disciples before Jesus sent them out.

And He called the twelve together, and gave them power and authority over all the demons and to heal diseases. And He sent them out to proclaim the kingdom of God and to perform healing. Luke 9:1-2

GIDEON

When the crowd and its needs became overwhelming, the loaves and the fish were all the disciples could see, but that is certainly not all they had. Like Gideon centuries earlier, they had the assurance of being called by God and given power and authority. They had a reserve of spiritual power to accomplish divine tasks, as well as the authority to tap into that power any time the need arose.

The combination of these two spiritual gifts—power and authority—is incredibly important. If you have power but no authority to use it, the power is wasted. It's like having a million dollars in the bank but no one to approve your withdrawal. A useless fortune. Jesus granted the disciples (and us) the authorizing clout to use the power inside.

Power—*dynamis*, (pronounced DEE-nah-mees)—capability, ability, power potential

> Using information from the paragraphs above and the two definitions in the margin, create a one-sentence description of the relationship between spiritual power and authority.

Authority—*exousia*, (pronounced ex-oo-SEE-uh)—freedom of choice.

Retrieving and walking in the power you've been given is a daily require-ment for victorious Christian living. Otherwise, you're like Jude in the dollar store, despairingly clutching his two pennies. To get the remainder, he needed only to ask for my help or at least be willing to pass the bill my way. Then he had to be willing to receive the gift that I was eager to give.

Accessing the power within you is as simple as prayerfully asking God to unleash it into your experience—day by day, moment by moment—then being willing to "walk by the Spirit" (Galatians 5:16). He releases power to you throughout the moments of your day. As you remain obedient and dependent on Him, you will experience the effects of power-filled living.

> In Luke 9 compare verse 6 with verse 12. In the latter verse, what might have caused the disciples to forget the gifts they had been given?

Personalize your response. If you had to pinpoint something that most often distracts you from remembering and using your unseen supply, what would it be?

Maybe if the disciples had recalled the gifts they'd been given, they would have felt confident before the hungry crowd. Instead of trying to send the people away or attempting to get away themselves, they would have stood their ground—fish and loaves in hand, power and authority in their hearts, smirk of confidence on their faces—as they anticipated what God would accomplish on their behalf.

At the close of our third week together, I'm asking you to do what the disciples did not: remember the unseen supply within you instead of being distracted by what's around you. There is a power source in your soul that you have the authority to access through Christ—anytime, anyplace. Your resources are in your relationship with Jesus Christ. Tap into the power source, and prepare to be surprised by His ability operating in your life.

Today my #LessonsFromGideon are:

Session 4
VIEWER GUIDE

Our God is _____. He's _____-_____.

Ephesians 3:20

"It is His patience that _____ our sinful hands and led us to the doorstep of His _____ that we might enter in."

Exodus 34:6/Nahum 1:3

1 Timothy 1:16

1 Timothy 1:15

1. He _____ Me

1 Peter 3:20

Genesis 18:26-33

Jonah 3:4

Titus 2:11-12

2 Peter 3:9

Genesis 4:26

Judges 17:6

1 Timothy 1:13-14

To access the video teaching sessions, use the instructions in the back of your Bible study book.

2. He _____ Me

    2 Thessalonians 2:13

    1 Timothy 1:12

1. He Saved Me (Justification)

2. He Changes Me (Sanctification)

3. He _____ Me (Location)

"God does not choose a person because he is _____ but by His choosing of him He makes him _____. " Augustine

4. He _____ Me (Fortification)

week

four

DAY 1
THE GOD OF PATIENCE

Gideon's story highlights many elements of God's character. Seeing the Midianites unleashed on the Israelites shows the judgment of God. Raising up a deliverer reveals the mercy of God. The victory of Gideon's 300 over the enemy points to the power of God. But the story unmasks another divine attribute that should make us eternally grateful: the long-suffering nature of God. "Therefore the LORD longs to be gracious to you, and therefore He waits on high to have compassion on you" (Isa. 30:18).

If there's anything I can say about my own relationship with Him, it's that He has patiently pursued me, consistently tolerating my spiritual mood swings. He hasn't been unnerved when I've taken longer than I should to obey Him, believe Him, or trust His guidance. Instead of swift justice, He has extended mercy, offering me chance after chance. No one else in the entire world has dealt with me so kindly. So patiently.

So far, what circumstances can you recall from the story of Gideon that reveal God's patience?

Grace = getting what you don't deserve.
Mercy = not getting what you do deserve.

Patience expresses itself by tolerance, offering favor, extending opportunities over long periods of time. This is why God's patience is most often described as "long-suffering" in the Torah and is frequently paired with the attributes of grace and mercy (Ex. 34:6; Num. 14:18; Ps. 86:15).

While you've been in this study, how have you seen the long-suffering of God demonstrated to you?

LORD, IT'S ME AGAIN

When last we saw Gideon, impending battle was thick in the air. He was down to God's desired allotment of 300 soldiers, and was preparing to somehow marshal his sparse forces against the Midianite thousands.

As I mentioned during our video session, we are going to take a break from our regularly scheduled program to highlight the times that unsure, hesitant Gideon received confirmation from God. In all three encounters we'll see a bright spotlight shining on "the God who gives perseverance and encouragement" (Rom. 15:5). What great reassurance for all of us (see me raising my hand?) who aren't always quick on our spiritual feet.

Each of these passages marks the beginning of a dialogue between God and Gideon. Underline any phrases that stand out to you. In the margin record what these tell you about Gideon or about God.

(Gideon) Then he said to Him, "If now I have found favor in Your sight, then show me a sign that it is You who speak with me" (Judg. 6:17).

(Gideon) "If You will deliver Israel through me, as You have spoken, behold, I will put a fleece of wool on the threshing floor. If there is dew on the fleece only, and it is dry on all the ground, then I will know that You will deliver Israel through me, as You have spoken" (Judg. 6:36-37).

(Yahweh) "Arise, go down against the camp, for I have given it into your hands. But if you are afraid to go down, go with Purah your servant down to the camp, and you will hear what they say; and afterward your hands will be strengthened that you may go down against the camp" (Judg. 7:9-11).

What are some similarities between these passages?

What major difference do you detect between the first two passages and the last?

Within a span of two Bible chapters, Gideon needs confirmation for his divinely mandated mission three times. His insecurity is so evident that God initiates the third encounter Himself.

While these instances clearly pinpoint areas of overwhelming weakness in Gideon, they also underscore something else: God's knowledge of them, His willingness to deal with them, and His ability to use Gideon in spite of them. God doesn't scold or rebuke Gideon for his lack of confidence nor ignore Gideon's request for confirmation. He takes active steps to accommodate Gideon's hesitance.

If you are in a season of life in which you feel insecure or doubtful about God, His Word, or His calling on your life, how do you honestly feel God is responding?
- ☐ He is mad at me for taking so long to know for sure what He wants me to do.
- ☐ He loves me but isn't interested in the smaller details of my life.
- ☐ He still loves me but is frustrated and impatient with me.
- ☐ He knows me, understands my weaknesses, and is patient with my uncertainties.

You chose one of the options above as the way you think God responds to your insecurity. If you think about your selection carefully, you may find it indicates what your response would be if you were God. We often think that God deals with us in the same way we deal with others. So since we'd be frustrated and impatient with a friend or spouse who was consistently unsure or apprehensive, we expect God must feel the same way about us.

Based on Judges 6:39, which of the above options do you think would best describe how Gideon thought God would feel about his need for confirmation?

Then Gideon said to God, "Do not let Your anger burn against me that I may speak once more; please let me make a test once more with the fleece, let it now be dry only on the fleece, and let there be dew on all the ground."
Judges 6:39

GIDEON

For Group Discussion: Many Christians view God as demanding and impatient with little tolerance for human insecurity or weakness. How do you think this view is shaped? What can be done to combat it?

God's patience = restraining power
#LessonsFromGideon

The phrase "slow to anger" is frequently coupled with "abounding in steadfast love" (Ex. 34:6, ESV) through the Old Testament. This steadfast love is the *chesed* love of God: the sure mercies of God involving the grace, favor, and mercy of God toward men.

Based on the fact that God initiated the third conversation, what can you infer about how God felt?

I'm so grateful to see Yahweh in light of Gideon's story. I can't begin to tell you how often I've harbored deep-seated insecurities. I remember feeling particularly unsteady when my twenties gave way to my thirties. I fervently prayed, much like Gideon, that God would give me clarity about the ministry to which He was calling me and the life He had given me as a wife and mother. Mind you, this was well after God had already gone out of His way to affirm His work in my life in so many obvious ways. Yet I still felt so incompetent, ineffective, and weak, and I wanted His confirmation ... again. I talked with Him day in and day out, and get this: He heard, showed up, and answered me in a way that was unmistakably reassuring ... again. He patiently worked with my weakness.

Yahweh's relationship with Gideon is not an exception; it is an example that reveals to us what we should expect in our relationship with Him.

THE POWER TO BE PATIENT

We don't typically think of those in authority as patient. Powerful people can be most intolerant of others' weaknesses. So the Holy One choosing to bear with us through our reservations—even through our sin—is a concept almost too difficult to absorb. But unlike human power, God's power walks in concert with extreme patience. In fact, His power enables him to exercise unbelievable restraint. That's how He shows His authority—not only by what He can do, but by what He chooses not to do. Hallelujah!

The lavishness of God's patience is equal to the vast abundance of His power. The latter is the support system of the former. So if you ever question God's patience toward you or are constantly looking for the proverbial "other shoe to drop," you'll have a long time to wait. His mercy is everlasting.

This is good news because it means your actions or inaction cannot stir God to impatience. Discipline, maybe. Correction, maybe. Fatherly action, maybe. But not impatience. We cannot weaken His divine long-suffering because it is dependent upon His power, which is unending and abundant. When God does choose to unleash His wrath and/or judgment, it is based on His own divine will, not a knee-jerk reaction born out of frustration.

How would you describe the connection between God's power and His patience?

Choose one of the three cases in the margin to study. Answer the following questions about the passage.

What phrase denotes God's long-suffering?

How did His long-suffering translate as grace and/or mercy in the participant's experience?

How can you see that God clearly restrains Himself in this story?

What personal application can you draw from the story?

Three Cases
1. Nineveh in Jonah 3:4-10
2. Noah in Genesis 6:5-8 and 1 Peter 3:20
3. The Israelites in Numbers 14:11-13, 20, 26-31

WHAT ABOUT YOU?

As we become more aware of how undeserved God's patience is, the natural outcome should be a deep desire to obey and trust Him. We should never see His patience as an excuse to spiritually slack off, thinking He must be cool with whatever level of effort and faith we feel like exerting. Our response should be to live thankful, expectant lives. And not only that, His gift of patience to us should compel us to want to give it to others. He Himself will empower us by His Spirit to do it (Col. 1:11).

But the fruit of the Spirit is … patience. Galatians 5:22

God's graciousness allows us to be ourselves and feel accepted. Giving this same gift to others will impact our relationships. Ask the Lord to help you relate to Him as the patient, loving Father He is and to give you the power to be patient with others as well.

Today my #LessonsFromGideon are:

GIDEON'S GIFTS

One of my greatest joys in ministry is corresponding with those the Lord places within my ministry path. Emails, blog comments, and Twitter posts allow me to hear from people I might never meet face-to-face. And inevitably, one of the most frequent questions I'm asked is "If I feel called to ministry, how do I start pursuing it?"

While my answers vary based on the specific circumstances, my response normally includes some variation of this idea: "Give back to the Lord the desires and gifts He has given you and then trust Him to use them when and how He chooses."

> **Write the words from this statement that resonate with you the most. Why?**

> **Which portion is hardest for you? Prepare to discuss this with your group.**
> ☐ offering your gifts back to the Lord
> ☐ offering your desires to the Lord
> ☐ trusting Him with when your gifts are used
> ☐ trusting Him with how your gifts are used

So Gideon said to Him, "If now I have found favor in Your sight, then show me a sign that it is You who speak with me. Please do not depart from here, until I come back to You, and bring out my offering and lay it before You." And He said, "I will remain until you return."
Judges 6:17-18

Not long after his first conversation with God began, Gideon realized this meeting was more than a human exchange. He sensed destiny fluttering in his heart, even though this whole encounter was still shrouded in fear and uncertainty. Gideon needed reassurance. So he made a deal.

> **From Judges 6:17-18 in the margin, record the details of Gideon's request.**

> **What was the angel's response to him?**

Surprisingly, the *Malak Yahweh* (angel of the LORD) wasn't upset by what Gideon proposed. He agreed to wait. Yep, you heard me right. God agreed to wait ... on a man. He wanted to receive the gifts that Gideon would prepare. He cared about Gideon's gifts—just like He cares about yours.

Gideon's gifts were physical, tangible goods: bread and broth. Ours can be tangible too, like money or time. But often our gifts are the intangible talents and passions He has given us to serve Him. Have you ever felt as though the gifts you have or the positions to which you've been called are meager compared to others? I have. In fact, my desire to study Gideon's story in the first place was largely born out of my own insecurities and weaknesses. I've often fallen into the pit of comparison, which can sometimes leave me with a smothering sense of fear, inadequacy, and lack of confidence.

Maybe you know this feeling too. It's understandable. We glorify the gifts that hold a microphone, while we downplay those that are done behind closed doors holding a dustpan. Yet some of the most faithful, effective Christians I know are those who are living out their quiet calling to the few in their home, to their fledgling church, or to the homeless under a bridge in their city. Nothing is meager or insignificant about that.

> **What do you sense God asking you do as you go through this study? What gifts has He given you to accomplish this task?**

To read more about Gideon's gifts, see Digging Deeper IV on page 104.

Now there are varieties of gifts, but the same Spirit.
1 Corinthians 12:4

GIVING GOD OUR GIFTS

Open your Bible to Judges 6:19-20 and notice the progression of events. I'll meet you back here when you're finished.

Did you see the four important steps in giving our gifts to God? Gideon prepared the gift for the stranger, then he presented it to Him. After that, the angel asked him to put it down and then pour it out.

> **List the three elements of Gideon's meal (verse 19).**

4 Steps in Giving Our Gifts to God:
1. Prepare it.
2. Present it.
3. Put it down.
4. Pour it out.

Nothing was fast about this food. No stores nearby where Gideon could quickly purchase his meal. Gideon's meal was homemade in the purest sense of the word. He killed the young goat himself, kneaded the unleavened dough for the bread, and whipped up the broth—all from scratch. It was an extravagantly sacrificial meal, given Israel's current state of deprivation. It required time, effort, and energy to prepare. It was a sacrifice.

Many Christians don't want to start here. They balk at doing the hard work involved in the preparation process. But you cannot expect God to use what you have not taken time to prepare. Dedicating the time to hone your gift will help you be ready when He opens the opportunity before you.

What practical things could you do to prepare the gifts the Lord has given you?

When the time was right, Gideon had to be willing to bring out the meal and give it to the angel. Prepared gifts cannot serve their purpose if they're kept in hiding. They need to be brought out and presented to be used.

Prepared gifts don't work unless they are presented gifts.
#LessonsFromGideon

I know many people who have done the diligent work of preparing their gifts but are too steeped in doubt or fear to bring them to God. So they're left holding good gifts that are not being used for God's purposes.

Which part of this process is hardest for you?
☐ having the patience to faithfully prepare your gift
☐ having the courage to present your gift to God

Explain your answer.

PUTTING IT DOWN, POURING IT OUT

When I give a gift to a friend, I have a definite idea of how I hope it will be used. I picture people enjoying the new kitchen appliance or wearing the nice blouse I found at a local boutique. At the very least, I certainly don't want them re-gifting it. I think Gideon probably had a certain expectation after going to all the trouble of preparing such a fine meal for his heavenly visitor. But the angel didn't lick his lips and dive into the meal as Gideon might have suspected. Instead he chose another, very strange way of accepting the gift. He told Gideon to "take the meat and the unleavened bread and lay them on this rock, and pour out the broth" (Judg. 6:20).

Ummmm. Excuse me, sir? I've just slaved over this exquisite meal for hours. You want me to do WHAT with it?

Yes, the angel told Gideon to release the very thing he'd so painstakingly prepared. To put it down. And pour it out. Two actions that would never be at the top of any chef's list when serving a meal to a new friend.

After so many hours of preparation, what would your response have been to this treatment of your gift?
☐ Ignore the command.
☐ Reluctantly obey.
☐ Take it to someone who will appreciate it more.
☐ Immediately and gladly obey.

What was Gideon's response (end of verse 20)?

Releasing our gifts back to the Lord for Him to do with as He pleases is difficult and humbling—especially since we often harbor desires of what we hope He'll do with them once we finally present them.

When we present our gifts to God and it becomes clear that what He intends for us to do is put-it-down and pour-it-out, we can become frustrated. That's because without even knowing it, we've placed a demand on God to use our gift in a certain way. "God, I'll do THIS if you promise you'll do THAT." When we find out He never agreed to such a negotiation, we can come unraveled.

From Gideon's story we learn an important lesson: the best use of our gifts is seldom what we imagined. If we'll put them down and pour them out, we'll be surprised at God's unconventional ways of using them.

Have you ever been disappointed at how God has asked you to use your gifts? How have you seen God use your life in a way other than you intended?

When Gideon obeyed God's command, his gift was met with a stunning divine display. An average rock became an altar. "Then the angel of the LORD put out the end of the staff that was in his hand and touched the meat and the unleavened bread; and fire sprang up from the rock and consumed the meat and the unleavened bread" (v. 21).

With that, Gideon's gift became a sacrifice, an aroma of worship sweeter to God than any he could hope to produce. Had Gideon's gift gone as he'd hoped, it might have been tasty, but it wouldn't have been a sacrifice to God.

As we traverse the story of Gideon together, I have no doubt that God's Spirit is going to show us the power in these four steps of divine gift-giving. I want to encourage you, sister-friend, to trust Him with your gifts. Nothing is commonplace or meager with what you have to give, as long as you …

Prepare it.

Present it.

Put it down.

Pour it out.

Today my #LessonsFromGideon are:

GIDEON'S GIFTS

The idea of ghosts and apparitions was not uncommon in the Jewish culture of Gideon's time. Thus his need for assurance in Judges 6:17 that this was *Malak Yahweh* and not some other spirit was understandable. Yet several details about Gideon's gifts reveal that while he may still have been uncertain, he at least suspected this was Yahweh's angel.

First, Gideon used the Hebrew word *minchah* when referring to his gift, a term most commonly used in reference to a sacrificial offering. When coupled with the animal sacrifice, *minchah* usually referred to the official meat and drink offering.[1] Gideon knew sacrifice was God's currency for meeting with humanity. Thus, his choice of elements possibly transcends mere hospitality and carries a holy connotation.

Second, the elements Gideon offers are closely linked to the sacrificial system of worship established by Moses. While Israel had moved away from obedience and consistency in their sacrifices, Gideon was likely familiar with them. His culture was filled with attempts to obtain relationship with God through sacrifices. The system for atonement in Israel called for 1,273 public sacrifices each year.[2] His choice of meat and unleavened cakes was probably deliberate. The correlation becomes even more clear when he lays down his gifts on a rock—a noted act of sacrifice.

When the angel requested broth be poured out, he was reaching back to one of the most conspicuous features of sacrifice in Scripture, shown by Jacob in Genesis 35:14. He also pointed forward to the new covenant under Jesus Christ. "The broth, or juice, denoted the blood, the life of the animal; and this was to flow over the extemporized altar on which the flesh and the bread were laid. A rude, but expressive, forecast of the Supper of the Lord—the unleavened bread of sincerity and truth, the flesh of the Lamb slain from the foundation of the world which is meat indeed, and the Blood poured over the world which is the drink indeed!"[3]

Another important insight lies in the order of the exchange between Gideon and the angel. Moments after Gideon sacrificed his gifts on the rock, peace was established. Gideon built an altar called "The LORD is Peace" (Judg. 6:23-24). Establishing peace was the final step before Gideon was allowed to move forward in his divine assignment.

In the ancient sacrificial system, the meal offering came directly before the peace offering—the final, sealing atonement for sin and celebration of reconciliation with God. All of the other offerings climaxed in the peace offering, which symbolized communion and peace with God. Gideon's gifts were symbolic of the pathway his own life was following.

From hesitating to holy. From cowardly to courageous.

DAY 3

THE FLEECE, THE DEW, AND THE THRESHING FLOOR

Today's title sounds like the Chronicles of Narnia, doesn't it? But it's not a C. S. Lewis novel—just a day in the life of a timid farmer-turned-military-leader. If you didn't know much about Gideon before, you still probably had heard of his fleece. It's nearly as famous as David's giant and Jonah's fish. Yet the fleece incident has given ol' Gideon a bit of a bad rap. His audacity to put God to the test seems unwise and potentially even arrogant.

Was he right or wrong to ask this type of favor? Well, let's see.

> **Ask the Lord to give you a fresh perspective and understanding of Judges 6:36-40. Take time to read it in your Bible. It's OK. I'll wait.**

Remember, divine patience is the foundation for all of Gideon's exchanges with God. Here, in this one conversation, where God not only answers Gideon's first request but his second, God's patience is staggering. Two factors make God's willingness to respond unbelievable. First, it is clear that Gideon already knew he had been called, Who was calling him, and precisely what he was being called to do.

> **In the margin mark the portion of Judges 6:36 that reveals Gideon's certainty about what he had been called to do and who was calling him to do it.**

Second, while support from others is not always a sure sign of God's favor, Gideon must have sensed confirmation in Israel's response to his leadership. With a piercing blow on the horn from a man of no repute among his people, more than 30,000 Hebrews left their homes to follow Gideon into war. Yahweh allowed the crowd's unified assent. This should have quelled Gideon's insecurity. Yet despite these holy gestures, Gideon needed more. So, he set out a fleece.

> Then Gideon said to God, "If You will deliver Israel through me, as You have spoken."
> Judges 6:36

Put yourself in Gideon's sandals. In what ways do you think his insecurity and timidity may have caused him to downplay the credibility and importance of the two significant assurances he had already been given? Consider the following questions in light of your own relationship with God.

How do you normally deal with confirmation God gives you about His will for your life?

Are you easily satisfied when He extends Himself to you or do you always need more?

What are the reasons for your response?

THE FLEECE

Scholars say fleece was very likely a fabric worn to shield oneself from the cold night air and the heavy dew that fell in Palestine. When Gideon slept in it, dew would have collected on it and it would have needed to be wrung out in the morning. So while the fleece later gathered theological implications (which we'll look at tomorrow), Gideon's idea for this transaction with God probably came from his common nightly experience with fleece.

From Judges 6:36-40, describe the difference between Gideon's first request and the second.

Gideon started off with a request for one sign, which quickly multiplied to two. Isn't that the way it goes? We intend to ask God for a quick, easy confirmation to quell our concern. But somehow, we still find ourselves wanting and needing more. So more requests follow. And more. And more.

The fact is, needing a sign indicates a weakened faith in a believer. Gideon's inability to be reassured wasn't a lack of communication on God's part. The problem was with Gideon. His fledgling faith needed to be matured.

Your faith can be stronger than a fleece.
#LessonsFromGideon

Recall a time when God confirmed His Word yet you still sought subsequent confirmation from Him. Record your thoughts.

What spiritual principle can you draw from the two statements of Jesus in the margin.

A believer seeking confirmation is not the same as an "evil generation" needing to be convinced of Christ's lordship, but the principle is still the same. Our God wants to be taken at His Word (faith), not relegated to performing signs (fleeces) to be believed.

TO CONFIRM OR NOT TO CONFIRM

To be fair, I'm not sure that Gideon's fleece request was unfounded or uncalled for. Think about it. Up until that point, the battle had been merely a thought in his mind; now the tremendous task was at hand. The venomous enemy had gathered (Judg. 6:33). People's lives were at stake and the battle was imminent. With no military training or previous experience to speak of, Gideon found need of assurance before launching into the biggest assignment of his young life.

Gideon was demonstrating a certain amount of wisdom and maturity by his desire to receive assurance before lunging over the precipice into God's purposes. He was cautious and careful, not wholly doubtful and disbelieving. Gideon was not expressing unbelief in God, which would have surely kindled God's anger, but rather an imperfect faith that needed to be strengthened. This is beautifully described by one scholar as the "honest doubt in which faith lives."[4]

What are some of the differences between seeking confirmation from God because of caution and seeking it because of doubt and unbelief?

If you are seeking confirmation right now, which of these options best describes your inquiry?
☐ I have full faith in God in this matter but just want to be cautious and careful before moving forward.
☐ I'm struggling with doubt and am not sure He has given me the strength to accomplish the task.

For Group Discussion: Compare and contrast Gideon's encounter with God and Moses' encounter in Exodus 4:1-14. Why do you think God became angry with Moses but not with Gideon?

What's important here is the heart behind the request. Remember that Gideon's circumstances were vastly different from ours. We have what he did not—the closed canon of God's holy Word and the indwelling Holy Spirit.

GIDEON

For another instance of confirmation comparable to Gideon's fleece, see Genesis 24:12-14 where Abraham's servant seeks a wife for Isaac.

Not only that, but "the national oracle was far away at Shiloh. He had grown up in a semi-heathen community, and his views were narrow and confused."[5] He had been taught to believe in Baal, so his relationship with Yahweh was young and inexperienced, given that he'd only met Him days or possibly weeks before. God knew these things and endured with Gideon based upon this understanding.

Guess what? God knows us too. Individually. Personally. He is well aware of our understanding and the depth of revelation He's given us regarding His will, both general and specific. He knows the sensitivity of our heart, our true desire to know His purposes, and our willingness to follow through on the clarity He gives. He relates to you and me today based on these facts.

To confirm or not to confirm is often our concern. I believe we can ask God for clarity in the face of challenge when our request comes from a true sense of faith—a faith that needs only to be strengthened—but not when we know we have purposely ignored what He has already revealed. Gideon's method suited him in light of his circumstances, but continuing to set out fleece after fleece is inappropriate and unnecessary in light of ours.

I do believe that confirmation is one of the great mercies God extends to us. Why? Because He isn't hiding His plans from us. More than anyone, He wants us to know His will. "If anyone is willing to do His will, he will know of the teaching, whether it is of God" (John 7:17).

I have more than one example of God reassuring me about His purposes for my life in undeniable ways. He is merciful when He sees our insecurity. So ask Him for confirmation when it comes from an honest desire to move forward in obedience, but don't count on signs to do what His Word and His Spirit have already been given to achieve. They are enough. If you look carefully, you might find He's already given you every confirmation you need.

Today my #LessonsFromGideon are:

THE "DEW" AND THE "DO" OF HEAVEN

I like signs. When I'm driving to a location I've never been to before, I appreciate every single indicator that tells me I'm headed in the right direction. Each new marker builds my confidence and buoys my certainty. So even if we're still on the fence about whether Gideon's request for a sign was a tad misplaced, I still get it. Don't you?

Yet, I can think of numerous times when I've passed a sign too quickly and didn't pay attention to what it said. As Gideon sat beside the bowl filled with liquid proof of God's response, I'm fairly certain that he didn't catch the full significance of the fleece incident. I bet the water dripping from his hands after wringing out the fleece matched the sweat dripping from his brow as he contemplated the marauding forces approaching. The enemy was closing in, and his troops were preparing to head out. A lot was going on in his head and his heart when God poured out dew, first on the fleece and then on the ground.

If Gideon was intended to gather any more profound meaning from these divine exchanges, he likely missed it. He had no way of mining the treasure of this divine interaction like we do with Bible in hand and God's Spirit in heart. Today, I want us to look at some of the nuances of Gideon's fleece—specifically, what it tells us about God and the application we can make to our lives.

THE "DEW" OF HEAVEN

One of my favorite parts of the day is the early morning when the sun is just rising and the day smells crisp and fresh. As many days as I'm able, I like to jog through my neighborhood to take in all the moist air. I marvel at many things—the bursting colors of the trees and flowers, the sounds of birds chirping above, and the feeling of moisture brushing across my ankles as I walk through patches of grass. I often wonder about that dew. If it didn't rain last night, how'd it get there?

Throughout Scripture, dew is used as a sign of divine grace and favor (Prov. 19:12). Dew is frequently a symbol of a special endowment of God's kindness and approval expressed to His people. Like dew, grace is a surprising gift that cannot be handmade or manufactured. God extends it to

GIDEON

When the dew fell
on the camp at night,
the manna would fall
with it.
Numbers 11:9

So Israel dwells in
security, the fountain
of Jacob secluded, in a
land of grain and new
wine; his heavens also
drop down dew.
Deuteronomy 33:28

Now may God give you
of the dew of heaven,
and of the fatness
of the earth, and an
abundance of grain
and new wine.
Genesis 27:28

humanity as a miracle from on high. And I believe the Bible's usage of the symbol gives us license to apply a deeper meaning to our lives than Gideon was able to understand.

> **Consider the verses in the margin. In what ways do the references to dew accompany or highlight God's kindness to His people?**

In His first exchange with Gideon, God poured out dew upon the fleece and not the ground around it. His gift wasn't meager or stingy. It was so robust that the fleece was waterlogged—a stark contrast to the dry, parched threshing floor underneath it. The difference was noticeable and staggering. The fleece was soaked and soggy; the ground, arid and scorched. If we can take any lesson from this, it is that the dew of heaven makes its target different than its surroundings.

> **How should the grace and favor bestowed on believers refresh them? How can it make them different and distinct from the *ground*—the culture of which they are a part?**

> **Is the dew of God's grace clearly seen in your life by others? Pinpoint three specific ways that you are clearly dissimilar from the world around you.**

The dew of heaven makes us different.
#LessonsFromGideon

1.

2.

3.

If you cannot pinpoint
any differences,
consider what this
probably tells you
and discuss it with
someone in your group.

Like the refreshing scent of a dewy morning, where the grass is damp and the air sweet, our souls are to be constantly refreshed by the invigorating, thirst-quenching dew from heaven, and we should be so clearly marked by grace that it is apparent to all those around us.

THE "DO" OF HEAVEN

Now let's look at part two of the fleece episode. Gideon turns the tables on God and asks for the fleece to be dry and the ground around it wet. Since fleece is naturally absorbent, Gideon may have thought the first day's result was simply normal. Dew on the ground would naturally have dried up more quickly than dew on the fleece. Maybe this wasn't such an adequate answer after all, he reasoned. So he chose a more miraculous test the second time to reassure himself of God's answer.

Before we move forward, I want to remind you of something: don't forget that Gideon has been tagged with a new name. He is Jerubbaal—the Baal fighter. His primary mission, aside from disarming the Midianites, was to dismantle the nation's misplaced loyalty to their idol. "Jerubaal" means "Let Baal contend" for himself. Jerubaal (Gideon) is now a living reminder of the impotence of the idol. So let's take a closer look at one particular element of Baalism he was fighting against.

Baalism was based on a belief system that said miracles were impossible. As a boy, Gideon was probably taught that God may have created everything, but the world was kept functioning by the simple, impersonal processes of nature. The universe, a Baalist would subscribe, was self-sustaining, with no eternal Being actively involved in supporting and maintaining it. While they believed it possible to stimulate or manipulate nature/Baal to respond in a certain way (see margin note), they firmly believed that the world and its happenings were independent of God's involvement.

This made the personal, intimate relationship that Yahweh offered to Gideon contrary to his Baal-instructed mind. He had never felt a need to pray for certain things, because the processes that nature put in place were set and could not be altered. To a Baalist, it seemed quite plausible for dew to be retained in a naturally more absorbent fabric like fleece. This was nature's way. But to change the natural order—to see a dry fleece lying on a patch of dew-infused ground—would refute the processes of logic … and one of the most critical elements of Baalism.

What type of internal transition must have been happening in Gideon's heart for him to even consider making this second request to Yahweh?

In 1 Kings 18, Elijah confronted the Baalists on Mount Carmel. Their attempts to coerce Baal to send fire from heaven would not have been viewed as a request for a miracle but rather an attempt to stimulate Baal/nature. "Within their system of belief, this was not a miracle, but a 'scientific' way of manipulating forces to achieve a desired result."[6]

What deeper, more critical statement was God making to Gideon and to His people by answering this request? Respond in the margin.

As I mentioned at the end of our first week of study, Baalism sounds like such an ancient and distant religion that we tend to think our modern society has no trace of it. But consider the many things we don't take to God in prayer because we've grown accustomed to the usual processes we experience daily. This reveals the crafty spirit of Baalism running rampant in our modern culture, cloaked in the guise of humanism. Even God's people have been duped into believing that either He will not really do anything on our behalf or that He doesn't need to because certain things just happen anyway. So we pray less and less about the details of our lives.

But Yahweh was not and has never been Baal. He could and would intervene in a very personal and intimate way in Gideon's life. Miracles were possible because there was a Miracle Worker. The "Baal Fighter's" response from Yahweh would be proof of that. God could "do the dew" anyway He wanted. No problem.

Are there any areas of your life that you no longer talk to God about because you feel like "that's just the way things are"? If so, what areas are they?

You, sister, are a "Baal fighter" like Gideon. Your life and mine are to be proof that Yahweh exists and is not only able but willing to intervene in our lives in personal, miraculous ways. Fight the spirit of Baal, my friend, by "let[ting] your requests be made known to God" (Phil. 4:6). Let the dew of heaven reinvigorate you and inspire you to stand against this deceiving spirit in your family, church, and community. Then, like Gideon, prepare to be astounded at all that your God will "do" for you.

Today my #LessonsFromGideon are:

DAY 5
FAITH SQUARED

It was a cold winter morning and I was a bit sullen. Some work I'd been trying to accomplish wasn't … working. I felt dispirited and incapable. A cloak of discouragement began to drape its dead weight around my tender soul, suffocating any creative juices. My husband could see the gloom all over my face when he came home. He took one look at me and knew that I was struggling again.

Kindly, tenderly, he said, "Nuh-uh. Don't even let yourself go there. Remember how the Lord confirmed His Word to you? The calling He placed on you? I was there. I remember it clearly. Don't let a little difficulty cause you to forget." With that, my dear man recounted for me the details of the event I mentioned to you a couple days ago in your Bible study lesson. For a moment, under the mounting pressure of an impending deadline, I'd forgotten. It took another person—a person who had been there to see it firsthand—to remind me of what the Lord had done.

> The heartfelt counsel of a friend is as sweet as perfume and incense.
> Proverbs 27:9, NLT

DO YOU HEAR WHAT I'M HEARING?

Not much is written about our dear Purah in the Bible. He was Gideon's servant (Judg. 7:10), most likely enlisted to bear his armor and accompany him into battle. Perhaps he was one of the ten guys Gideon had recruited to help him overthrow the Baal altar in his father's shrine (6:27). He is mentioned only one time by name in the Bible. On this particular evening, Purah's role expands. He steps from the shadows onto center stage as Gideon's companion and confidant. He will accompany Gideon on one last adventure before the battle begins.

> According to Judges 7:9-11, what did the Lord assure Gideon about again?

> Did God require Gideon and Purah to go into the camp before the battle began?

> Finish the sentence: Gideon is to go into the camp with Purah only if …

> Now the same night it came about that the LORD said to him, "Arise, go down against the camp, for I have given it into your hands. But if you are afraid to go down, go with Purah your servant down to the camp, and you will hear what they say; and afterward your hands will be strengthened that you may go down against the camp." So he went with Purah his servant down to the outposts of the army that was in the camp.
> Judges 7:9-11

What was the result of his experience there (v. 11)?

After all of the divine exchanges you've studied this week between Gideon and Yahweh, why might this one underscore the patience and kindness of God even more than the others?

What might have been some of the benefits of Purah's presence with Gideon during this adventure?

Earlier that day, Gideon's army had dwindled to a mere 300. Any confidence he may have had from the whole fleece incident was quickly evaporating. So he took God up on His offer for yet another confirmation before launching the attack.

Use your imagination to picture these two men descending the darkened hillside, traversing the two miles that separated the enemy's camp from theirs. Intense darkness lay like a thick blanket across the valley, the stillness punctuated only by their quickly beating hearts.

The closer they got to the camp, the more clearly they could see the adversity before them. Any hope that the threat might not be too bad disappeared as they came face to face with a vast swarm, appearing "as numerous as the sand on the seashore" (v. 12).

Gulp. Their hearts beat faster.

Name two upcoming situations in your life that appear more intimidating the closer they get.

What details of these challenges cause you the most concern and anxiety?

Like my task at home on that cold morning, we can often become more and more overwhelmed the longer we grapple with a challenging situation—whether it's a decision that needs to be made, a conversation that needs to be had or a task that needs to be completed. But sometimes another person's confidence is all you need to stay your course and continue with the mission as planned. A friend's encouragement can help keep your head in the game when you would rather forfeit. This could have been the very reason for Purah's presence that night.

> **Name some people who have seen what God has already done for you or who you trust enough to tell about your previous experiences with God.**

For Group Discussion: During this study, God will give you direction, stir conviction, and offer encouragement and comfort. How can your group walk together in accountability after this study ends to remind one another of what God has accomplished?

I'M DREAMIN'

As Gideon and his comrade approached the Midianite camp, they might have seen the following setup: "The women, children, camel-drivers and camels, would have the centre of the interior. In front and in rear, and as wings on either side, would be the companies of the armed men."[7]

One of the first tents they would likely have come to on the outskirts of the encampment would have been housing men prepped for war. Gideon and Purah stumbled on a tent where two men were relaying their thoughts to each other before retiring for the night.

If you think about it, this fact alone is an enormous miracle. The probability that they could creep into the camp unnoticed and then happen upon the exact tent in which these men were talking about Gideon is unfathomable. Read Judges 7:13-15 below.

> When Gideon came, behold, a man was relating a dream to his friend. And he said, "Behold, I had a dream; a loaf of barley bread was tumbling into the camp of Midian, and it came to the tent and struck it so that it fell, and turned it upside down so that the tent lay flat." His friend replied, "This is nothing less than the sword of Gideon the son of Joash, a man of Israel; God has given Midian and all the camp into his hand." When Gideon heard the account of the dream and its interpretation, he bowed in worship.

Imagine how surprised Gideon must have been to hear his and his father's names coming out of a Midianite's mouth. How could they possibly have any opinions on his ability as a military leader? Clearly Yahweh had already begun to intervene by spreading terror over the enemy camp to prepare for that night's ambush. Gideon and his men were being set free from fear while their enemies were being divinely paralyzed by it.

> For the Hebrews, dreams carried special significance. Go back to the passage you just read and underline the phrases "barley bread," "the tent," and "turned it upside down."

Let's explore each of these elements. Barley bread was the bread of the poor. It had become the meal of the oppressed Israelites who had fallen prey to the devastating yearly pillaging of the Midianites. In the dream, a loaf of this bread tumbled from a precipice into the camp and flattened *the* tent, which is distinctly different from saying *a* tent. The men discussing the dream were in *a* tent, but only the commander had *the* tent—the headquarters of their intel and the center of their military operations. The tent was not just crushed, it was turned "upside down," signifying a complete reversal of their prosperity and well-being.

> Beside the portions you underlined in the passage, write these words next to the parts of the dream they correspond to. "Israel," "Midianite headquarters," and "reversal of well-being."
>
> What did the dream mean to Gideon and Purah?

TWO HEADS ARE BETTER THAN ONE

If this revelation didn't give Gideon complete assurance, then nothing would! The enemy not only knew his name but was already predicting Israel's victory. And now, instead of being reassured by God while alone in a winepress or on a threshing floor next to a damp fleece, he was with a friend who had heard and seen it all too. If Gideon's confidence were to wane again, Purah would be there to remind him of this epic evening.

Has God ever used you to be a backbone of confidence during times of insecurity for others?

How can you take this role more seriously in your friendships?

Do you see someone struggling right now who could benefit from your reminder of what God has done in her life?

We don't know for sure that Purah ever had to remind Gideon of what happened that night. But we do know the Bible doesn't record another instance where Gideon asked God for confirmation again. It seems that his confidence had been adequately boosted by this final, divinely orchestrated event. Yahweh, long-suffering and compassionate, had gone out of His way to tend to Gideon's weakness and had even put him in the company of another for moral support along the way. Filled by God's Spirit, Gideon was about to gather his men and move forward into an epic night that would change all of their lives forever.

It was now or never.
So, now it must be.
"Arise, for the LORD has given the camp of Midian into your hands" (Judg. 7:15).

Today my #LessonsFromGideon are:

Session 5
VIEWER GUIDE

Romans 10:17

Judges 7:15

1. Begin the Battle on _____ _____.

Joshua 6:20

Judges 7:15

2. Face the Battle from a _____ of _____.

Judges 7:16

Ephesians 2:10

3. Advance into the Battle from Your _____ _____.

Judges 7:16

Judges 7:21

1 Corinthians 12

Judges 7:19

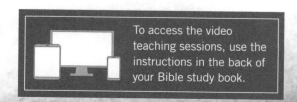

To access the video teaching sessions, use the instructions in the back of your Bible study book.

4. Approach the Battle at just the _____ _____.

Judges 7:20

5. You Win the Battle by Using the _____ _____.

Judges 7:21-22

UNUSUAL WEAPONS

Our last video session together was one of my favorites. Going into battle with Gideon was an adventure we won't ever forget, huh? The Lord sent them in and brought them out unscathed and intact. He'd won a spectacular battle on behalf of His people and He'd equipped them with the most unusual weapons with which to do it. While a sword and shield or bow and arrow may have seemed a more suitable way to surround the enemy camp, Gideon and his men were sent into the dark night with an odd arsenal of what appeared to be nothing more than common kitchen tools.

Do you recall the three weapons Gideon's 300 used in battle (Judg. 7:16)? How would you like to go in to a battle, outnumbered 450 to 1, with a torch, a trumpet, and a water pitcher? These weapons serve as a very tangible reminder of the entire premise of Gideon's story—that God uses "the weak things of the world to shame the strong" (1 Cor. 1:27, NIV). Up until now we've only seen hints of this biblical truth through a timid farmer rallying his troops and seeing his army whittled down to 300.

GIDEON

For other instances of unusual weapons, see Judges 9:50-54; 14:6; 15:15

Now we're encountering it head-on as the soldiers have gone to war with this seemingly useless weaponry.

Interesting, isn't it, that no record exists of any one of the 300 men refusing to use their paltry instruments. No one disdained them or tried to exchange them for real weapons before the battle began. No one called Gideon a fool for instructing them to be used. They just grabbed the horns, clay vessels, and torches they were given and went to do battle. Can you imagine the amount of faith they must have had in Gideon to trust him, to follow him toward the marauding forces of Midian with these odd implements clanking at their sides?

Sure you can, because you've known what it's like to trust God when He's asked you to use His weapons to fight your battles. Consider some of the common weapons we often prefer to use: human strength, natural talent, power, human reasoning, wealth, personal reputation, etc.

What would you add to the list of common weapons?

When disagreements erupt, financial debacles arise, physical disturbances ensue, mental exhaustion surfaces, or dreams feel threatened, we want to bring our muscle to the mix. But when God's Spirit gently reminds us of the uncommon spiritual weapons we've been given—and of the spiritual realities at play within every circumstance of life—He wants us to step out with a firm resolve and dependence on Him, using different tactics than usual. Consider some of the spiritual weapons God has given us to use against enemy attacks: the Holy Spirit, prayer, God's Word, faith, humility, weakness, truth, and praise.

Uncommon weapons are needed for uncommon battles #LessonsFromGideon

What would you add to the list of divine weapons?

What is your usual response when the Spirit prompts you to fight using these spiritual weapons?
☐ I hesitate because I'm unsure they'll work.
☐ I use them but complain while I'm doing it.
☐ I use them but keep worrying at the same time.
☐ I ignore God's suggestion altogether.
☐ I trust Him and use His weapons.
☐ I do something else.

Let's face it, spiritual weapons are unusual to use when other tactics seem so much more rational given your circumstances. But that's if "you are looking at things as they are outwardly" (2 Cor. 10:7). Sometimes only spiritual weapons can get the job done.

THE BATTLEFIELD

No matter how sharp the sword or wide the shield, Israel would not have benefited from using traditional weapons the night they met Midian in battle. Their attempts to use them would have fallen flat. Why? Because only the weapons God had specifically given for this battle were suitable. His are the only weapons that will work for us as well—in battles that are much more spiritual than we often realize.

> In the chart below, record three difficult scenarios facing you right now. List your natural response. Then ask the Holy Spirit to reveal what divine weapon He might want you to use from this point forward.

Spiritual warfare is a conflict waged in the invisible spiritual realm that manifests itself in the visible physical realm.

SITUATION	NATURAL WEAPON	SPIRITUAL WEAPON
1.		
2.		
3.		

Every physical reality contains a spiritual root. So if you deal with only the natural reality, using natural resources, you will never drill down to address the spiritual reality. You may be able to patch up the symptoms for a while, but the real problem will remain unsolved and simmering.

That's the enemy's plan—to talk you into ignoring the divine reality occurring beneath the surface of your difficulties, leading you to downplay the significance of your spiritual weapons.

What "logic" does the enemy typically use against you to disguise the spiritual nature of your struggles and to mask his role in them?

THE WEAPONS OF WARFARE

The pitchers Gideon's 300 carried were inexpensive vessels normally used to hold water. In this case they each held a lamp lit by oil and fire, concealing the light during their approach to the enemy camp, shielding it from the elements of wind and the night air. Not until Gideon ordered his men to announce their surprise attack were they to smash their pitchers, letting the light of the torches shine brilliantly against the darkened sky. Made of clay, the pitchers shattered instantly.

The pitchers' value was twofold. First, the pitchers' importance didn't come from their composition but from their contents. The vessels needed only enough material and maintenance so the burning flame inside could be protected, ready to be unleashed at the sound of Gideon's battle cry.

> A vessel's value is not determined by its composition but by its contents.
> #LessonsFromGideon

Prayerfully consider 1 Corinthians 6:19 in light of the significant points in the previous paragraph. When you're ready, answer the following questions:

How is your body like the 300's pitchers?

How can you be sure your pitcher does its job well?

How is the Holy Spirit like the 300's torches?

Right now, how is the care of your pitcher assisting in its protection of the torch inside?

Second, the pitchers' importance came from their weakness. Listen carefully now, Sister. The pitchers used by the 300 were frail. Easily breakable. But the weakness was not a liability; it actually made them effective. If the pitchers were made of an indestructible substance that wouldn't shatter at once, the torches would have remained concealed. The pitchers' frailty benefited their ultimate purpose—allowing the light to be seen. Each vessel's true strength was displayed when it was cracked open and the light inside pierced through the darkness to shock and blind the enemy.

We are "like a broken vessel" (Ps. 31:12). The weaknesses we often despise are required for the light of Christ to be seen and for the darkness around us to be dispelled. Without the limitations and deficiencies of our vessels, we would not serve our purpose well.

Your weakness is not a liability. It is one of your greatest assets. God's presence and power are best seen when our large, impressive personalities aren't getting in the way. So welcome His light into your weakness, and let it shine, let it shine, let it shine!

Consider the New Testament passage in the margin. Mark each portion that relates to the vessel and the torch. Use the space below to record the meaning for you as the Holy Spirit applies this truth to your life.

What are some of the weaknesses in your life through which the power of Christ is most clearly seen? How can these be "weapons" for your warfare?

For God, who said, "Light shall shine out of darkness," is the One who has shone in our hearts to give the Light of the knowledge of the glory of God in the face of Christ. But we have this treasure in earthen vessels, so that the surpassing greatness of the power will be of God and not from ourselves.
2 Corinthians 4:6-7

Gideon's epic victory was won with uncommon weapons and, as a result, became a constant reminder about the power of God over Israel's enemies. For years to come, this triumph would be remembered as the night when God fought on His people's behalf (Ps. 83:9-12; Isa. 9:4; 10:26). If anyone dared question the power and ability of Yahweh, he need look no further than Gideon and the 300's weapons to be silenced.

Yes, indeed, it's uncanny what God can do with a willing soldier, her broken vessel, and the blazing flame of His own fire.

Today my #LessonsFromGideon are:

FINISHING WELL

My favorite events to watch in the Olympics are the track and field relays—not just because of the ultimate dash to the finish line, but because of the action within those twenty-meter spaces known as the exchange zones. Races are often won or lost not by the runners' speed in their leg of the relay, but because of their baton exchange.

Many a team has lost the gold medal by dropping a baton or bobbling a handoff. This critical zone can't be taken lightly. Every step; every second counts. Every runner must do her part, then let someone else carry it forward to finish the race.

> **If you've ever worked hard to pursue a dream or aspiration, then sensed God telling you to pass the baton to another, how did you respond?**

> **In the Christian race, why do you think the exchange of the baton is so vital, and why do you think people find it difficult?**

Think back to our favorite fleece-testing Bible character. Could Gideon have been so caught up in the victory over Midian that he didn't realize his leg of the race may have been over? Scholars are divided on exactly when Gideon's spiritual decline began, but its underpinnings may possibly be tucked in between the lines of Judges 7:23-24 (see margin, page 127).

Had Gideon been commissioned by God to gather these tribes and pursue the enemy remnant? Or was the battle over for him, his leg of the race complete? We can't know for sure, but the mere fact that God's guidance is so conspicuously omitted from this point on in Gideon's story gives us a hint of something going awry. God had spoken freely and frequently up until this point. But now? He is silent. What began as a divinely ordained undertaking seems to be turning into a mission for personal retribution (see 8:19).

Gideon wanted revenge. The consequences of this change in motivation will reverberate throughout the rest of his account.

BEYOND BOUNDARIES

Scripture gives us several hints that Gideon's divine assignment had been completed. First, the last of the Midianite soldiers had fled far beyond the usual limits of pursuit to the safety zone called Karkar (8:10-11). The kings went back to wearing their "crescent ornaments," a sign they were going back to normal, assuming they were no longer in danger. A second hint appears in the Israelite soldiers being called to rejoin Gideon's ranks.

> In the margin compare Judges 7:23-24 with the first recruitment of soldiers from 6:34-35. What three tribes were mentioned in both?

☐ 1.   ☐ 3.

☐ 2.

The soldiers that rejoined Gideon's battalion "probably consisted of the twenty-two thousand who had been eliminated in Judges 7:3 and those ninety-seven hundred who had been sent back to their tents for lapping water like dogs in v. 8."[1] Gideon forgot (or ignored) that Yahweh had already sent these men home! A smaller army assured that all the glory for victory would be directed toward Yahweh, but now the army had swollen again and Yahweh's goal was hampered.

We unearth a third layer of insight in the original wording used by the author of Judges. It's a bit heady, but I know you can handle it. Take a moment to concentrate on 6:34-35.

> In 6:34, underline the words "the Spirit of the LORD came upon Gideon." Now, draw an arrow to connect this phrase to Gideon's action.

In the original language the grammatical phrasing purposefully cements the connection between Gideon receiving the Spirit and then acting. The blowing of the horn and the response of the Abiezrites were both directed and empowered by Yahweh. At first glance, the next four tribes seem to gather for the same reason—the Spirit's leading—but again, the original language, allows us to understand more fully.

> Circle "he sent" and "he also sent" in verse 35. Then draw lines to the tribes involved each time.

[margin]
²³The men of Israel were summoned from Naphtali and Asher and all Manasseh, and they pursued Midian. ²⁴Gideon sent messengers throughout all the hill country of Ephraim.
Judges 7:23-24

³⁴So the Spirit of the LORD came upon Gideon; and he blew a trumpet, and the Abiezrites were called together to follow him. ³⁵He sent messengers throughout Manasseh, and they also were called together to follow him; and he sent messengers to Asher, Zebulun, and Naphtali, and they came up to meet them.
Judges 6:34-35

Unlike the direct connection between God's empowering and Gideon's actions in verse 34, the grammar in verse 35 reveals a disconnect between Yahweh and His Judge. This twofold break in the narrative—twice saying "he sent"—shows that these last tribes joining Gideon's ranks, although graciously allowed by Yahweh, may not have been a consequence of Yahweh's direction. In other words, after the initial gathering of the Abiezrites, Gideon should have gone confidently into war with those who responded to the sound of the horn. Instead, he hesitated and insecurely summoned a larger group.

> **Think how Gideon handled tearing down his father's idol (6:27). Comparing 6:34-35, what pattern of behavior do you see unfolding? (Respond in margin).**

Gideon had a habit of stepping beyond the prescribed direction of God to pacify his insecurity and timidity. So when God defeated the Midianites that fateful night, Gideon seemed to slip back into his old pattern of padding his self-doubt with excess resources. Would Yahweh have wanted Gideon to summon back the very resources He'd sent away earlier? Instead of continuing to trust in the one true God, Gideon reverted back to his previous reliance on human strength. More troops began to take the spiritual place that had been carved out for faith and dependence on Yahweh.

> **Are you ever inclined to pacify your insecurity instead of staying inside the boundaries set up by God? If so, what are some of the ways you have done this?**

I'M FINISHED?

What's important is not whether we can pinpoint exactly when Gideon stepped beyond his assignment. We'll see another possibility later this week. What's important is making sure we don't do the same.

Will we choose to be content taking a task up to a point and then, at God's bidding, walk away or pass on the baton to another? When you've dreamed up the organization, laid the foundation, crafted out its mission, and worked diligently to get it up and running—then you sense God's Spirit whispering, "Enough"—it can be hard to let go. Instead of gracefully, even cheerfully stepping aside, we can be tempted to greedily cling to ministries and positions, aspirations or dreams long after we've passed through the zone of divine exchange. What if finishing well means ... not finishing?

The biblical character David might have an answer for us. He yearned more than anything to build a house for God. His intentions were pure; his purpose honorable. Yet even this noble aspiration was met with a heavenly halt. God instructed the prophet Nathan to tell David he would not build the house; one of his successors would build it instead. So David had to choose how to respond: selfishly hang on to the baton or prepare to pass it on?

> **What did David do in response to God's instructions? (See 1 Chron. 22:11, 14a, 19 and 29:2-4.)**
>
> **How would you describe David's attitude? What led you to this conclusion?**
>
> **How did David treat his successor?**
>
> **What did David emphasize to Solomon and the people of Israel?**

Finishing well could mean not finishing.
#LessonsFromGideon

Even today, 2,500-plus years after its construction, the temple is historically referred to as "Solomon's Temple." But what of David? He didn't build it, but he did prepare for it. Solomon's success was built on the strong foundation of his father's provision. Had David not done his part, Solomon could not have successfully done his. David accepted his boundaries and excelled within them. Then he cheerfully passed on the baton. He knew how to be finished … even when the project wasn't.

I wonder how many divine missions, mandates, and ministries have been aborted by selfish, insecure Christians who refused to do their part wholeheartedly and then relinquish the task to the next person God had anointed with His favor to run the next leg of the race.

I wonder how different Gideon's story might have turned out if he had been satisfied with simply doing what God had empowered Him to do.

How will your story change if you do?

Today my #LessonsFromGideon are:

FRIENDLY FIRE

My sons have a hard time celebrating each other. When one of them has been successful in the classroom or on the court, the others often wince to hear celebration and admiration being dished out on their brother. Instead of adding to the congratulations, they find it easier to point out something that could have been done better or differently.

- "That's the only A you've made on a vocabulary test this year."
- "That shot would have been 'all net' if your arch had been better."
- "You could have run a bit faster on that touchdown."
- "You should have worked out those math problems in your head like I can instead of having to do them on paper."

Why is it so hard for us to genuinely affirm another's success? Maybe we imagine God has an enormous "blessings basket," and if He takes one out to give to someone else, it somehow lessens those available for us.

Why do we become riddled with envy as we stand outside the spotlight others are enjoying? There in the shadows, we force a halfhearted smile, while secretly wishing we were in the limelight of their achievement. We feel left out, insecure, somehow minimized. Then our undue insecurity breeds scrutiny. We become judgmental, finding fault even if there is little to be found, offering our finicky, cynical opinion.

Who do we think we're fooling? Our true intentions give us away every time. Sooner or later the façade breaks down and our selfish and critical colors shine through.

Ephraim's did.

> Then the men of Ephraim said to him, "What is this thing you have done to us, not calling us when you went to fight against Midian?" And they contended with him vigorously.
> Judges 8:1

RAINING ON MY PARADE

What was Ephraim's beef with Gideon (Judg. 8:1)?

Why might this be a surprising response based on the events in Judges 7:24-25?

Ephraim had not been included in the initial rout of the Midianites. When Gideon was first commissioning assistance, he didn't personally summon them to participate. When he did call on them, it was only as a last resort because the enemy was fleeing through their territory. So, yes, they assisted in cementing the victory, but they were not content to stand just outside the spotlight of the success claimed by Gideon and the 300.

Get the picture here: the air of victory was hanging over the valiant 300 battalion like a banner. The battle had been won, and the whole war appeared to be sealed now that the Midianite leaders, Oreb and Zeeb, were killed. Gideon and his troops were ecstatic. Yahweh had won the battle for them, no doubt about it. Victory was sweet.

Then, like rain storming down on a Macy's parade, the proud tribe of Ephraim launched a verbal attack that quickly dampened the soldiers' festive mood. Smiles faded. Tensions rose. Cheers of victory subsided. Hurtful discouragement settled in the place where happy excitement had been.

Let's be honest: the reason this lesson hits such a nerve is because we've probably been on both sides of the criticism coin—offering unnecessary, belittling comments one day, then being on the receiving end of them the next. We know how it feels to give them and how it aches to receive them.

So why do we do it? And how can we stop it?

> **Put yourself in Gideon's sandals. Recall the last time you were on the receiving end of a dose of criticism. What effect did it have on you?**

Now, sit in Ephraim's camp. Think back to the last time you, even inadvertently, rained on another's parade. Then consider the following questions:

What made you feel justified in your comments?

Why did you find it difficult to affirm this person?

How did your comments affect him/her?

How did being critical make you feel about yourself?

CRITICAL CHAOS

This passage marks the first dispute in the Book of Judges between two of Israel's tribes, and their dissension would be costly. The bickering among God's people cost precious time and energy that could have been reserved for more important tasks. As we'll soon see, their reserves of food, supplies, and vitality were already running low. So instead of wasting effort on an internal argument, they should have been safeguarding their resources for the common mission at hand.

> How are the troops described in Judges 8:4?

> How do you think dissension contributed to this?

> In what ways do critical people drain you?

> In the margin list the important tasks that may be going unattended because of your zapped reserves.

The chaos created by criticism can be staggering. While Ephraim picked their fight, operation Conquer Midian had to be suspended. The panic-stricken, war-torn enemy troops escaped to the east and made it to the watering holes of Karkor before Gideon and his men could catch up.

> On the Geography of Gideon map in the back of your book, search for the arrow pointed toward Karkor and write "70+ miles."

While Karkor cannot be pinpointed with certainty, it was at least 70 miles from where Gideon's army first began its pursuit. God's people were fighting while the enemy was gaining ground. Think of all the ways you've seen the enemy gain ground when discord has developed among God's people.

THE ROOT OF IT ALL

> What does the similarity between Judges 8:1 and 12:1 in the margin tell you about the tribe of Ephraim?

> In the following two paragraphs, underline reasons Ephraim was critical of others.

The Ephraimites were proud, self-centered, and irritable. They carried an enormous sense of entitlement due to several factors. First, their

Then the men of Ephraim said to him, "What is this thing you have done to us, not calling us when you went to fight against Midian?" And they contended with him vigorously.
Judges 8:1

Then the men of Ephraim were summoned, and they crossed to Zaphon and said to Jephthah, "Why did you cross over to fight against the sons of Ammon without calling us to go with you? We will burn your house down on you."
Judges 12:1

important cities of Bethel and Shiloh were key rallying points for the nation. Since Shiloh was the religious center for Israel, Ephraim felt a uniqueness and special closeness to God.

Second, as the central tribe, they were located away from the border territories that had been the first to be ravaged by Midianite attacks. Their land and their people hadn't suffered the same losses other tribes had. They felt special and exceptional, not damaged and devastated.

> **How have you seen the sentiments you just underlined play into a critical nature you've encountered in another person?**

See Digging Deeper V on page 135 for another factor that contributed to Ephraim's superiority complex.

Does our disapproval of another's decisions or actions stem from a perceived personal closeness to God? We can begin to think our spirituality is more in tune and on target, leaving us licensed to judge them with the weight of God behind us. Instead of love and tolerance, we express anger and unkindness.

What about the false sense of superiority that sometimes arises when we see the hardships or consequences others are dealing with that we've escaped? Instead of humbly counting it to God's grace, we make sweeping, heartless assessments of others from an unfortunate sense of entitlement.

> **Have you seen either of these affect your treatment of others? If so, how?**

FROM COMPETITOR TO ENCOURAGER

Maybe Gideon was aware of how much time and ground they were losing, or maybe he could see the morale of his troops fading. But no matter the reason, wisdom fueled his response to Ephraim's childish antics.

> **How did Gideon's response to the Ephraimites in Judges 8:2-3 diffuse the situation?**

Compare Gideon's response to Ephraim to Jephthah's in Judges 12:2-4. How were they different? What was the result of each response? Respond in margin.

Instead of caving to the cheap shot, Gideon chose a humble response peppered with diplomacy. He minimized his own achievements and high-lighted theirs. Using poetic language, Gideon asserted that the killings that day of Oreb and Zeeb ("the gleaning of Ephraim") were far more impres-sive than Gideon's success the night before ("the vintage of Abiezar").

Abiezar was the name of Gideon's clan within the tribe of Manasseh.

Jephthah wasn't wrong; he just wasn't wise. Only someone who has consciously chosen humility and the quiet strength of restraint will be able to respond to critics as Gideon did. He shrewdly quelled the fiery contention among his kinsmen for the sake of the greater mission at hand.

What would it look like for you to use Proverbs 15:1 in your most trying relationship today?

A gentle answer turns away anger, but a harsh word stirs up wrath.
Proverbs 15:1

As you close your lesson, turn to Philippians 2:3 and Romans 12:10 and prayerfully consider them. Then resolve to quell the spirit of criticism in yourself and others today. When you desire to be critical of others, take that as your cue to bless and encourage them. Instead of becoming defensive, reacting negatively, or internalizing any criticism leveled at you, respond in gentleness and love as the Spirit empowers you to diffuse the situation in wisdom.

Today my #LessonsFromGideon are:

EPHRAIM & MANESSEH

A millennia before the time of Gideon, Joseph brought his sons Manasseh and Ephraim to their ailing grandfather's bedside. The time had come for the family birthright to be passed on (Gen. 48). As was customary, the eldest was set to receive the primary blessing. So Joseph strategically placed Manasseh near Jacob's right hand of favor and Ephraim on the left.

For reasons known only to the patriarch, Jacob switched his hands and thus the blessings. He crossed his hands, placing the right on Ephraim's head and his left on Manasseh's. With this one simple yet significant move, he passed over Manasseh for the primary blessing and gave it to his younger brother Ephraim. From that day forward, Manasseh's posterity took second place to Ephraim's.

Joseph was shocked. His knee-jerk reaction was to take his father's hand to move it from Ephraim's head to Manasseh's (Gen. 48:17), but Jacob refused. He hadn't made a mistake. He was aware of his actions and affirmed his choice of Ephraim.

Time would confirm that Jacob's selection had been rooted in prophetic foresight into Ephraim's future. During the wilderness wanderings, Ephraim's tribe would be more numerous than Manasseh's. Significant personalities, like Joshua, would emerge from Ephraim and their city Shiloh would be home to the tabernacle. When Israel entered the promised land, Manasseh would be divided in its inheritance of land, thereby weakening their resolve, while Ephraim would remain intact both in geography and power. Every Israelite, including Gideon, knew of Ephraim's position of superiority. This was one reason for Gideon's astonishment and disbelief that *Malak Yahweh* would choose him, a man whose family was "the least in Manasseh" (Judg. 6:15), to lead the crusade for freedom out of Midianite oppression.

A generation earlier Jacob himself had received the birthright and blessing instead of his older brother Esau (Gen. 25:29-34). Here again we see the pattern of Yahweh choosing the least likely and the weak over the strong. Even in ancient times, God selected unexpected people to demonstrate His power and serve His plan. It happened again when Gideon surprisingly rose from the lesser tribe to become a national hero.

Gideon and Ephraim had two things in common; first, they had both been called from second to first place. Second, they would each fall prey to a pride, selfishness, and sinister pretense that would sabotage their potential.

The constant heartfelt prayer of anyone God uses must be for continued humility and reliance upon the One who first commissioned them. Significance can far too easily turn to a self-centeredness and pride that will rot divine potential and incapacitate future use. We see it in Ephraim and, sadly, we will soon see it in our Gideon as well.

WEARY, YET PURSUING

Tired? It'd be understandable if you were. This week we've wielded unusual weapons in battle, stood our ground through the night in enemy territory, and dealt wisely with the criticism of others. Meanwhile, you've been living your own life filled with all the demands and duties that keep everything spinning. It'd make sense if you needed to draw a breath of relief.

> "I will strengthen you; surely I will help you."
> Isaiah 41:10

Gideon and his men most certainly did. They were "weary" (8:4). The adrenaline that had been pulsing through their veins was starting to wear thin, giving way to an awareness of empty tummies and fatiguing muscles. They hadn't eaten or slept in many hours, and they had no food or shelter to refresh them as they made their way east toward the Jordan River.

I'm very drawn to this segment of Gideon's narrative. I can relate to it, and I'm fairly certain you can too. These 300 men aren't made out to be superheroes with no need of rest. Even Gideon, the Baal-fighter empowered by Yahweh's strength, is included in their weary number. Their frailty is expressed more pointedly in 8:4-9 than anywhere else in the whole narrative. Yet there is no shame in their exhaustion; no embarrassment in their fatigue. Instead a hint of celebration and bravery is woven into the fabric of this text. Yes, they were weary, but they were focused on the pursuit at hand.

Circle the word "yet" in Judges 8:4. How does this word make all the difference in the verse?

> Then Gideon and the 300 men who were with him came to the Jordan and crossed over, weary yet pursuing.
> Judges 8:4

How do you feel most fatigued in your life right now?
- [ ] spiritually
- [ ] mentally
- [ ] other
- [ ] emotionally
- [ ] physically

Explain your choice.

How do you feel, or how do others make you feel, when you need a break because you are depleted and/or tired?

☐ guilty   ☐ ashamed
☐ embarrassed   ☐ sad
☐ understood   ☐ other

Write your own "yet" statement. Describe what you are weary from, yet what you are committed to do despite your exhaustion.

_____

_____ YET _____

_____

Gideon's story isn't intended to lead us to believe that God's empowerment will strap a superwoman cape on our backs. We shouldn't bear guilt when we feel fatigued. Admitting our depleted resources is not a cop-out or a sign of faithlessness. It just means that we need refueling as we continue to move ahead. But what if, when we look for refueling, all we get is refused? What will we do then?

ASSISTANCE PLEASE?

I recently spent eight days in a glorious ministry opportunity with women in New Zealand. I spoke ten times and loved every minute of it. But between the jet lag, late nights, and high energy I joyfully invest when teaching, I returned home gloriously spent.

Honestly, this weariness isn't too dissimilar from the way I feel at the end of a usual week in my life when I'm at home doing laundry, packing lunches, running errands, and breaking up sibling squabbles. The emotional, mental, and physical investment that women like us put into every aspect of our lives every week can be quite taxing. The more exhausted we feel, the greater our tendency to turn to something or someone else to refuel us. Read Judges 8:5-9 and answer the following questions.

To what two towns did Gideon turn for help?

What did he ask them for?

Did they help the 300?

What was Gideon's response?

Working tirelessly is not the same as working persistently.
#LessonsFromGideon

On the Geography of Gideon map, draw an "X" over these two locations, connect them with a line and write "4 miles" in between the two locations.

These two towns were both located in Gadite territory. Succoth was positioned very close to the Midianite region and would have known this enemy threat well. The 300 must have felt confident that these vulnerable towns would be grateful and eager to offer support. Boy, were they wrong.

Fearing the Midianites, Succoth and Penuel chose to err on the side of selfish and cowardly caution. If they helped and the enemy ever found out, their generosity might cost them. So they withheld support.

Imagine the disappointment of the hungry, depleted soldiers as they faced the reality of going on without food or supplies. First they had to go the four miles from Succoth to Penuel and then another twenty-five miles from there to Karkor.

We can relate. We have our own Succoths and Penuels. At the end of a long day, week, or activity when we've invested our full selves, we turn to certain habits, people, and environments for recharging. Certainly nothing is wrong with doing so, in most cases, but haven't there been times when we've found these options either unavailable to us or just somehow unsatisfying? What if home life is not the respite you were hoping for right now? What if the extra sleep doesn't quite fill the energy gap? What if your friend has her own needs and can't be the listening ear you want? What if your spouse is emotionally unavailable, your job unfulfilling, your coworkers unsupportive, or your ministry unexpectedly demanding?

What if our Succoths and Penuels don't help?

To what or whom do you usually look for refreshment?

In what ways do they give you what you need?

In what ways do they not give you what you need?

Succoth's and Penuel's refusals to help were an astounding affront to loyalty. In withholding assistance they were passively siding with the Midianites and disavowing their brotherly responsibility.

Which adjective would you use to describe the tone of Gideon's reaction (8:7,9)?

☐ understanding   ☐ mellow
☐ furious   ☐ irritated

What did he promise the leaders of the towns?

Gideon's response is understandable but not necessarily acceptable. Scholars are divided on whether this was authentic justice or personal vengeance. But one thing is clear: Gideon had changed. The meek, humble man who hesitated to fight the enemy of God's people is now intent on destroying his own. His focus has changed; his energy is now misdirected.

How have you responded to people or things that have not given you what you hoped they would? How is it similar or dissimilar to Gideon's response?

The text does not tell us where the 300's food came from, only that they found enough restored energy to go and "attack the army while the army was unsuspecting" (v. 11). While the text does not specify where they did receive help, the author highlights where they did not receive it.

    Maybe we should follow his lead and highlight where our help doesn't come from as well. Then we can be reminded of where it does.

Prayerfully consider the portions of Isaiah 40 written in the margin. What would it look like for you to live in light of these verses today?

What would waiting on the Lord look like practically in your life?

While the towns of Nobah and Jogbehah are mentioned in verse 11, we see no direct indication that they gave support to the 300.

The Everlasting God, the LORD, the Creator of the ends of the earth does not become weary or tired. His understanding is inscrutable. He gives strength to the weary, and to him who lacks might He increases powers. ... Yet those who wait for the LORD will gain new strength. Isaiah 40:28-29, 31

THE PASSION TO PRESS ON

I can't help but jump over to a New Testament passage as we close today's lesson. The apostle Paul penned a letter to the church at Philippi using athletic imagery that paints a great picture for weary warriors.

Forgetting what lies behind and reaching forward to what lies ahead, I press on toward the goal for the prize of the upward call of God in Christ Jesus.
Philippians 3:13-14

Underline key words that are descriptive of athletics in this passage in the margin.

Write the two things that Paul says are necessary in order to press on.

1.

2.

Disciplined runners consistently clear their heads and focus fully on the journey ahead. Are their muscles tired? Yes. Are their lungs strained? Yes. But can they continue? Yes, because their passion and zeal for the goal supersedes the strain. The goal beckons them onward. Passion doesn't negate weariness; it just resolves to press beyond it.

Passion doesn't negate weariness; it just resolves to press beyond it.
#LessonsFromGideon

So, today, release anyone or anything you've positioned as "Succoths" and "Penuels" in your life. Recommit yourself to a continued dependence and fellowship with the Lord, asking Him to give you what only He can—a passion that will ignite your heart for His purposes.

He can do it, you know?

He can and will stir your heart and awaken your soul with a passion that pushes past weariness. Then you'll be equipped to passionately pursue the goal for the upward prize of God in Christ Jesus.

Pushing past weariness is possible. So don't stop now, Sister.
Whatever you do, don't stop now.

Today my #LessonsFromGideon are:

THE DOMINO EFFECT

I'm a bit embarrassed to say it, but I just recently learned how to play dominoes. From my grandparents. I sat around their dining room table, frantically trying to keep up with the math accumulating around the branches of the domino tree we were creating.

Up until then, I'd only used dominoes for one purpose: lining them up, tapping the first one, and then watching the row tumble down all the way to the end. One tackled the next—each submerged under a flood of momentum.

Submerged.

Underneath.

Momentum.

I can relate. I can clearly recall times I've allowed myself to get caught up in the moment, whether from circumstances or someone else's actions. Before I knew it, one action had led to a reaction—and then another and another—and, just like that, I was submerged under a flow of momentum that had taken me so far off course, I could barely recall where I'd begun or where I was supposed to be heading.

But you don't have to know how to play dominoes to understand the domino effect.

GOING DOWN

Gideon is off course. We can specifically pinpoint the turn in Gideon's heart from divine mission to personal vengeance here. He has tracked down the Midianite remnant at Karkor, successfully routed their army, and detained their infamous leaders—Zebah and Zalmunna. The time for their execution has come. But first, he asks them a peculiar question in Judges 8:18 (HCSB)—"What kind of men did you kill at Tabor?"

This is the first we've heard of a battle at Mt. Tabor (a major mountain north of the Valley of Jezreel), yet it must have borne extreme significance to Israel's natives. The king's response, while vague to us, carried enough familiarity to resonate in Gideon's soul: "They were like you, each one only resembling the son of a king" (Judg. 8:18).

Gideon's mind must have raced with sentiment and emotional angst as he remembered how his brothers had gone missing after the bloodbath on Mt. Tabor.

GIDEON

"They were my brothers, the sons of my mother! As the LORD lives, if only you had let them live, I would not kill you."
Judges 8:19

Who were the slain men (Judg. 8:19)?

That was it. The final domino collapsed, slamming Gideon into a sordid mission of revenge.

How does Gideon's statement give us a clue to his heart's motivation (v. 19)?

Yahweh's directives are no longer Gideon's primary concern. He is now making decisions based on the actions of others. What the kings had done becomes the stimulus for what he will choose to do. Gideon is driven forward not by the voice of *Malak Yahweh* but by his past pain and emotional devastation.

If they wouldn't have, he wouldn't have.

He has gotten swept up in the moment. He's off course. Submerged.

Underneath.

Momentum.

Consider your life in light of this discovery. Have any of your divine assignments taken a turn toward personal interests? If so, what circumstances have caused you to change your focus?

Complete this statement:
If _____ would not have done
_____, then I would not have
done _____.

THE SLIPPERY SLOPE

If you look carefully at the events before the deaths of the Midianite kings, you can see the dominoes falling down and Gideon falling away from the purposes that first brought him out from under the oak tree in the winepress. Answer the following questions based on <u>Judges 8:15-17</u>.

Where did Gideon go?

Who did he take with him?

What was his purpose?

Which option do you think best describes what's driving Gideon's actions even at this point?
- ☐ contending for peace
- ☐ judging his people
- ☐ fighting idolatry
- ☐ retaliating

Gideon hadn't been joking when he threatened to pay back the people who refused bread to his weary troops. With the two infamous kings of Midian in tow, he returned to Succoth with a carefully prepared list of the 77 elders who would taste his horrific, brutal vengeance (Judg. 8:14). He then proceeded to <u>Penuel</u>, where his thirst for retaliation escalated.

How does his actual punishment of the men in Penuel differ from what Gideon initially proposed (compare Judg. 8:9,17)?

Penuel was a fortress city on a hill overlooking Succoth, boasting a strong tower in which they arrogantly trusted for security. Not only did Gideon tear down their citadel, leaving the inhabitants vulnerable and exposed, he went a step further by massacring the city's leaders.

Next, he turned his attention to the two kings, <u>Zebah and Zalmunna</u>. The fact that Gideon would have them killed is not surprising, but the person he appointed to do it is. With the weight of the first two dominoes leaning into his soul, he decided these kings needed to pay dearly not just for their raids into Israel but also for killing his brothers.

Who did Gideon choose to slay the kings (8:20)?

DOMINO #1
vengeance against leaders at Succoth

DOMINO #2
escalated anger and violence in Penuel

DOMINO #3
disgracing the Midianite kings

Are you experiencing one or more "domino effects" in your life right now? If so, list them below.

For decades the tale of these revered kings would be told with admiration and honor around late-night Midianite camp fires. Dying at the hands of Gideon's teenage son, however, would rob them of that dignity. Any time their legacy was recounted, the kings would be humiliated, laughed at, and ridiculed. They knew it, and so did Gideon. He didn't just want them dead; he wanted them disgraced.

Gideon's malice toward his own natives and then to these kings shows an escalating pattern of vengeful actions that no longer have roots in divine will. Gideon is operating now on his own, reacting to the action or inaction of others instead of staying steadfast to Yahweh's instructions. The dominoes are tumbling, and Gideon is caught up in the downfall.

THE MISSING LINK

Gideon could have avoided this domino effect. And so can we.

What do you think could have kept Gideon on track?

The Lord has not spoken since Gideon first tasted victory in battle. Even more disheartening, Gideon has not asked Him to. The consistent conversation once indicative of their relationship has faded. Intimacy. Fellowship. Conversation. If anything is missing from Gideon's experience with Yahweh, this is it.

How can confidence and success become the enemy of our fellowship with God?

Remember how frequently and eagerly Gideon sought divine direction at the beginning of his story? When he was steeped in uncertainty about himself and his circumstances, he was desperate, diligent, and consistent about talking to Yahweh. But now he is neglecting that which gave him confidence in the first place. Continuing a vibrant fellowship with God would have kept him on course with divine purpose.

Take a personal inventory: How is your relationship with God affected when you feel weak and uncertain about yourself or a task? How is it affected when you are confident and secure?

Seeking God and His will must remain our constant desire and aspiration, even after we've begun seeing His strength demonstrated in our lives. Otherwise, we will be submerged beneath the momentum of human approval, momentary convenience, personal desires, or misplaced ambitions. When the dominoes of life cave in, our level of steadiness will be equal to our level of fellowship with the Father.

Consider Jesus. After all, there is no better illustration of someone staying true to the task at hand.

> Do not depend on your own understanding. Seek His will in all you do, and He will show you which path to take.
> Proverbs 3:5-6, NLT

How did Jesus' communication with the Father keep Him on track (Mark 1:35-38)? How did it affect His decisions about what to do?

Jesus was intent on doing the Father's will . . . and nothing else. So He purposefully and faithfully sought the Father for direction, and then stayed committed to the divine purposes for which He had been sent even if it meant disappointing a crowd of people to do it.

I need to take a cue from Him. How about you?

End this week of Bible study by reviewing the path Gideon's story has taken. Take note of the dominoes that fell in each lesson this week and how they eventually caused him to veer off course. Prayerfully consider what's happening in your life right now and then make a commitment to remain consistent in your conversation with and dependence on God. The courage, direction, and divine favor you'll receive from an ongoing fresh relationship with the Savior is exactly what you'll need to stay on track.

That's momentum worth being caught up in.

Today my #LessonsFromGideon are:

Session 6
VIEWER GUIDE

Deuteronomy 17:14-15

Joshua 24:15

1. Who or what has _____ in my life?

Judges 8:22

2. Who have I been giving the _____?

Psalm 75:6

Deuteronomy 6:10-12

Judges 8:23

1 Corinthians 2:1-5

3. Do you _____ glory back to God?

Judges 8:24-25

Deuteronomy 20:13-14

1 Chronicles 26:27

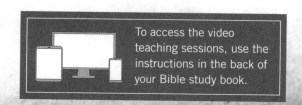

To access the video teaching sessions, use the instructions in the back of your Bible study book.

4. Are we keeping anything that _____ to God?

Judges 8:27: "It became a _____ to Gideon and his household."

Week six

NO OTHER GODS

Every year, my family heads east to Tyler, Texas, for a week at Pine Cove camp. I've gone to Pine Cove almost every summer of my life since I was five years old. Now my children look forward to it as well—seven full days of the same Christian activities and adventures I remember so clearly from childhood.

Time flies when we're immersed in all the fun of camp life. Zip lines, swimming pools, canoes, fishing rods, and campfires consume our waking hours (and the adults' fading energy) in every excitement-filled day. Before you know it, we're packing up to head home.

Last year, five days in, my oldest son walked over to me with a sullen expression, lamenting the swift passing of his long-anticipated camp week. He couldn't believe we had only two days left. By the time he finished his melancholy rant, tears were literally streaming down his cheeks.

Wiping them away, I said, "Honey, we aren't finished yet. You still have two days to go. Don't miss out on the excitement of what's still ahead."

Well, Sister, here we are in the final days of our study with ol' Gideon. When we first began, these six weeks stretched out before us like a never-ending sea of possibility. Now we're nearing the finish line together, but we aren't finished yet. Don't miss out on all that God has for you in this final week! Recommit yourself to the journey, even now.

Got your Bible and a pen ready? Grab them and let's dig in together.

GIDEON

THE INTERVIEW

Let's start with an interview. Picture us sitting together with two creamy lattes steaming before us. I'll ask the questions and savor my drink while you think of your responses. Take your time and when you're ready, write your answers below. For each question, list any habit, desire, person, or activity that fits the question.

Do you have to compromise your convictions to indulge any person or action?

Does anything weigh more heavily in your decision-making process than the voice of the Holy Spirit?

Do you have difficulty being content, joyful, or grateful without something?

Is there anything you cannot say no to, even when God is asking it of you for a season?

Do you automatically turn to something for comfort or relief when you're unhappy?

Does your mind immediately center on something as a solution when problems arise?

Now, take a deep breath, enjoy a taste of your latte before it gets too cool, and turn your attention back to Gideon's story. Your answers above are going to help us "do business" with the details of it in a very personal way.

Define the term *idol* in your own words.

KINGS AND THINGS

If I popped over to your house unannounced, I probably wouldn't find any carved images in your yard or next to your kitchen sink. You probably don't even use the words *idol* or *idolatry* in regular conversation. They conjure up thoughts of ancient times; things removed from our present reality. But idolatry is still very much alive today, no matter what modern terminology we attach to it. Modernized idolatry is still idolatry.

> **Think back to the video session. In the margin, underline any words or phrases in the verse that stood out to you during the teaching. Why do you think they struck a chord in your heart?**

Here, near the end of Gideon's story, Israel offers him a crown, and Gideon rejects it. These two actions are parallel rails on a track headed to a devastating destination. Over the next few days, our study will force us to travel down each one. As we do, we'll get a unique perspective on a spiritual dilemma that carries the same grave consequences today.

For now, let's plant our spiritual feet firmly on Israel's side of the tracks and see where it leads. Even before they asked Gideon to rule over them, Israel had been traveling down their side of the track for a long time. Their misplaced loyalties and misdirected desire for leadership are present throughout the Book of Judges. They had a pattern of looking for visible alternatives to their invisible suzerain. (Remember the Deliverance Principle on page 15?)

> **Think back: What was Israel's idol of choice when Gideon's story first began (Judg. 6:25)?**

Because a carved image could be seen, touched, and confined, the Hebrews found it easier to relate to the idol than to the one true God. So they gave to the idol the *hesed* (loyalty) that rightfully belonged to Yahweh. This is essentially what an idol is—*anything in the visible, created realm that begins to operate in a role that should be reserved for God.*

> **In what ways is this definition different and/or similar to what you first wrote?**

Then the men of Israel said to Gideon, "Rule over us, both you and your son, also your son's son, for you have delivered us from the hand of Midian."
Judges 8:22

ISRAEL OFFERS GIDEON A CROWN

GIDEON REJECTS CROWN

Modernized idolatry is still idolatry.
#LessonsFromGideon

GIDEON

For Group Discussion:
Discuss this statement from the video message: "We are not human beings having a spiritual experience; we are spiritual beings having a human experience." How does this relate to your definition of idol?

How do Israel's illegitimate worship of Baal and desire to make Gideon king fit into this category?

Review your answers from our interview. Mark any that fit into the definition of an idol.

Like ancient Israel, we often accept visible alternatives that divide our loyalty to our invisible yet faithful suzerain. When we can go to the drive-through window to get it, pick up the phone to order it, turn on the television to see it, run to the mall to buy it, or snuggle up on the sofa with it, *it* becomes easier to choose than God.

Israel chose Baal at the beginning of Gideon's story, then sought a human ruler toward the end of it. One was an image; the other was a human being—different, but the same. Both were intended to take the primary position of authority over the people, and they both created a fracture in the people's allegiance to Yahweh.

Both were idols that led the people into idolatry.

What if we got honest about what we're really dealing with? Let's call an idol an idol, then clear the deck of our hearts so we can get back to the relationship with Yahweh we were designed to have. You in?

Consider Romans 1:22-23. How have you seen this "exchange" happening in your life? What has been the result of it?

Professing to be wise, they became fools, and exchanged the glory of the incorruptible God for an image in the form of corruptible man.
Romans 1:22-23

CALL IT WHAT IT IS

As I mentioned in our video session this week, the Israelite leaders who came to Gideon with this proposal never actually used the Hebrew word for king (*melek*). In fact, they seemed to go out of their way not to. Yet no amount of linguistic acrobatics could disguise their intention. The job description was clear: they wanted Gideon to rule, and they wanted to set up a hereditary arrangement of succession—a dynasty to ensure that his sons would rule after him. They didn't come out and say "king," but that is exactly what they wanted Gideon to be.

Since Israel never had their own king before, the concept of hereditary succession was a prototype they'd witnessed in pagan nations.

Why do you think Israel's leaders might have deliberately chosen not to use the word *melek* in their proposal?

Do you find it difficult to use the word *idol* in relation to anything in your life? If so, why?

It's much easier to exchange this severe term *idol* for lighter, less harsh terms that are easier on the ears and less convicting to the heart. We call them bad habits, issues, obsessions, cravings. Carefully, craftily, we steer clear of saying *idol* just as Israel's leaders navigated around the word *melek*. But, honestly, we aren't fooling anyone any more than Israel did.

This week, let's allow the Holy Spirit to unveil the horrid statue of idolatry from underneath the cloak of fluffy, sweet phrases we've laid over it. It might cause a little emotional upheaval, but every ounce of freedom we'll gain will make every step worth it.

Since today's lesson serves as the launching pad for our entire study this week, keep the interview questions under consideration. If some of them were too difficult for you to answer on the spot or you have something else to add or change, come back and make notes that will help you get the most out of our final days of study.

Today my #LessonsFromGideon are:

GOOD TO BAD, BAD TO WORSE

I've never been to India, but one day I hope to see this distant and gorgeous land. My parents have. They traveled to New Delhi several times during my teenage years. Each time they came back with beautiful, ornate trinkets as gifts for my siblings and me to hold in our hands as well as some colorful stories to treasure in our hearts.

I remember hearing about the cows of India. Apparently they were everywhere—in backyards, on the side of the road, in the road. These animals, venerated as the sacred animal of the Hindu religion, graze and roam as they please.

We've got cows in my neighborhood. Right around the corner from our home, a fenced pasture boasts a handful of enormous cows my children enjoy watching. My husband likes cows too—when they're cooked medium-well beside a baked potato.

Yup, the Shirers like cows. Nothing wrong with them. But even good things become bad when they're elevated to an illegitimate position.

GOOD TO BAD

> Then the men of Israel said to Gideon, "Rule over us, both you and your son, also your son's son, for you have delivered us from the hand of Midian."
> Judges 8:22

A key word in Judges 8:22 will help us point a finger at the idols in our lives. While Israel never used the word *melek*, they did ask Gideon to *rule*. This clues us in to one of the crucial factors of idolatry. Idols control us and sit in the seat of ultimate authority in our lives. Whoever or whatever rules, no matter what we call it, is indeed king.

But does this only pertain to issues of addiction, immorality, and decadence? Are these the only things that can be idols?

Remember the definition for *idol* from our lesson yesterday. How would you explain the importance of the word *anything* in that definition?

That makes our ears perk up, doesn't it? Anything includes everything—even gifts God has given us to enjoy can take the wrong positions in our lives. In fact, inherently good things can often be the most harmful because they're sneakier. They lower our guard and relax our defenses. Under the guise of goodness, we leave them unattended in our lives until they rise to an inappropriate position of power.

- A successful career is a good thing ... until you're willing to compromise your values to sustain it.
- A committed significant other is a good thing ... until he consumes your attention.
- A padded bank account is a good thing, a blessing from God even ... until it becomes your source of security.
- Your favorite pastime is a great source of pure entertainment ... until it's all you ever think about and make time for.

Consider Israel's relationship to Gideon in light of this. How did it go from a good thing to a bad thing?

From your interview answers yesterday, choose two inherently good things and list them here.

Here are a few more examples. For each one, underline the positive behavior then circle the moment when it becomes inappropriate or negative. Use the journaling space under each to record how you may see a glimmer of it in your own life.

1. Cristal enjoys nibbling on tasty treats that nourish her body and delight her taste buds. But she's slowly become mastered by the desire to eat. Now she can't pass up a delicacy without putting her hands to her mouth, even if her stomach is filled to the brim, and even if feeling sick is only one bite away.

_____

_____

2. Michelle used to just enjoy shopping. An occasional afternoon stroll through a mall helped her relax and unwind. Recently she's gotten a bit obsessed, like when her favorite store doesn't have a gorgeous sweater she wants in her size.

She used to be able to walk away, but now she frantically calls other stores and searches online until she can find it. Her thoughts are consumed with owning it. When and if she finally locates one, she buys it without regard to her overtaxed credit card. She'll pay for it later. She always does.

---

3. Chastity is dating someone. It's about time! She's enjoying being wooed. During the third date, between the dinner and dessert course, the Holy Spirit began speaking to her heart. Her date's conversation and conduct was out of line with God's design. But instead of obediently telling him that their time together couldn't continue, she's kept quiet because she's enticed by the possibility of a future. It feels so good to be adored, dated, and smiled at like this. So she keeps going—one more date, one more month, one more year.

---

4. Haven's favorite television show took a sharp turn toward spiritually offensive things last season. Yet despite her disgust, she can't imagine not watching next season. Her children's sports schedule conflicts with the show times, so she sets her DVR to catch every episode. When the kids are tucked in bed, she curls up with her favorite blanket. The Holy Spirit convicts. She watches anyway.

Note in the margin ways you think these things have become "rulers" in these women's lives.

Have the two good things you chose from your interview begun to assume an illegitimate role of authority in your life? If so, how?

The clothes we enjoy, the food we need, the relationships we desire, the entertainment we like—while not wrong in themselves—can each become rulers, bossing us around and pulling us away from God's plans. They tell us what to do, when to do it, and how to get it done. Soon we look in the mirror and see a woman we don't even recognize anymore. She's going against her reason, her principles, and most devastatingly, the soothing conviction of God's Spirit. She's shackled to the very things she once right-fully enjoyed. God is not the ultimate authority in her life anymore.

BAD TO WORSE

Yes, good things can go bad, but also bad things can become worse. And they will. Two things idolatry is not: neutral or stagnant. The sins we entertain, the negative influences we accommodate, and the bad habits we indulge in become shackles that keep us from victorious living.

Let's look into Israel's history to get a better view of this. Read a very familiar passage, Exodus 32:1-5. Answer the following questions.

1. What did Israel want done?

2. What circumstances prompted them to want it?

3. Who did they ask to do it?

> Now on the same night the LORD said to him, "Take your father's bull and a second bull seven years old, and pull down the altar of Baal which belongs to your father, and cut down the Asherah that is beside it. ... Take a second bull and offer a burnt offering with the wood of the Asherah which you shall cut down."
> Judges 6:25-26

While Moses was up on the mountain conversing with Yahweh on their behalf, the people committed a horrendous sin that would mar the Sinai experience. Instead of waiting patiently for their leader to return with the purposes and plans of God, they chose to ask Aaron—the soon-to-be high priest—to invent a god for them. A century and a half before Gideon's time, they traded the invisible one true God for a visible substitute. A calf.

Now, let's draw a parallel between the Exodus 32 debacle and what we first discovered the people worshipping in Judges 6:25-26.

Compare passages. What connection do you see?

Bulls and calves were the cult animals of Baal worship. That the bull was seven years old draws our attention to two things: the maturity of the creature and the number of years Israel had been suffering under Midianite oppression. It wasn't a calf; it was a full-grown, adult animal. It wasn't a lifeless image but a breathing bull.

What began as an inanimate, fledgling calf in the time of Moses matured into a full-grown living bull in the time of the judges. Instead of worshipping a stationary yearling, God's redeemed people had graduated to the veneration of a living, moving, breathing, snorting adult animal.

What does this progression suggest to you about the potential of idolatry in our own lives?

Idolatry never stays small. What seems minor will spiral far beyond what we first imagined. It won't regress or retreat. Left unattended, it will grow and mature until its grip is beyond what we ever intended it to be. Calves become bulls. Never forget that.

Which of your answers from the interview are a testament to the bad-to-worse principle we've discussed here?

Sister, standing guard against idolatry requires that we give attention to even the good gifts in our lives, keeping them balanced under the authority and control of our God. Likewise, we must stand guard against the sins and hindrances that rob us of the abundant life we've been given. Doing so will set us free. And keep us that way.

Today my #LessonsFromGideon are:

FEELING FINE

Emotions don't have intellect. They don't think clearly or wisely. They can't make the best decisions and steer you in the most appropriate direction. They only want to be soothed and coddled, appeased and pacified. So it's rarely in our best interests to follow our feelings, using no other barometer to gauge our decision-making process.

I bet we could each share personal stories of times when our feelings have led us astray—how some internal pain, like loneliness, led to an immoral relationship. How jealousy led to people-pleasing. How fear led to procrastination. How we plugged the God-shaped hole in our hearts with a substitute because we *felt* like it was the right thing to do.

> **Keep your finger here and flip back to your answers from our interview. Which ones originated during a time of pain or emptiness in your life?**

Many of our idol hang-ups start this way—in places muddied by emotional difficulty. But if you'll step back again into Israel's camp around the base of Mount Sinai, you'll see that negative emotions are not the only kind that can lead us into spiritual adultery.

ON THE SIDE OF VICTORY

In the nearly eighteen months since Israel left Egypt, the Hebrews had seen Yahweh move in miraculous ways. The chapters leading up to Sinai read like a *Best of Wilderness Memories* book. If you look carefully, you'll notice that the low note of the golden calf incident occurred during a high note in their wilderness travel.

> **Open your Bible to the following chapters in Exodus, quickly scan the overarching theme (or just look at the chapter heading), and fill in the blanks.**
>
> **Chapter 14: God divided the _____ and the people narrowly escaped _____.**

Chapter 16: God provided _____ and meat so His people would not be hungry.

Chapter 17: God provided _____ to quench their thirst and gave them a miraculous victory over _____.

Chapter 19: God graciously began to give their leader the ten _____ and outlined the law for His people.

God's people had tasted the gracious kindness of their Redeemer in remarkable ways. Israel was experiencing a contentment and freedom they'd not known in centuries. In the midst of this emotional and national upswing, they ... uh ... gave their loyalty to another god. Really?

Nope, emotions, even good ones, don't steer you well.

In what ways can achievement, prosperity, and success contribute to a misdirection of loyalty?

We see this same pattern occurring in Gideon's era. It almost seemed admirable that Israel wanted a king and that they wanted it to be Gideon. Almost. For decades the tribes had been divided. Now, caught up in the current of national celebration, they desired to unite under one heroic leader—a leader whom God had called out of obscurity. So maybe, just maybe, we can find something to admire about their request, right? After all, things had been going so good.

Pinpoint at least two details you can recall from how Israel had seen God's hand of favor leading up to their request for king (Judg. 7–8).
1.

2.

When Gideon took the sword from his timid son on that final, fateful day (Judg. 8:21) and slew Midian's leaders, the victory for Israel was sealed. A wave of national congratulations swept the country. Their enthusiasm led them to make the hasty choice to ask Gideon to rule over them.

Emotions, even good ones, don't steer you well.

For Group Discussion: The Hebrews requested the golden calf when they become tired of waiting on Yahweh and Moses to finish their conversation on the mountain. In what way does impatience play a role in idolatry in the life of modern-day believers?

Turn back to your interview again. Which decisions originated during a time marked by happiness, success, or contentment?

Sure, gaping holes in our hearts can lead to idolatry, but there's another side to this emotional coin that can't be overlooked—the good side where we feel so secure, certain, and satisfied that we make hurried, thoughtless decisions just because it feels right in the moment. If we aren't on alert, we can get caught up in a current of self-confidence headed toward a deep ocean of idolatry.

FATHER KNOWS BEST

Israel was an emotional toddler, unable to corral its feelings (negative and positive), make wise choices, or maintain its ultimate allegiance. Yahweh knew this about His beloved, so a century and a half earlier, He had made provisions for this.

Read Deuteronomy 17:14-15a, where the Lord predicts the people's desire to have a king.
1. Why would Israel want a king?

2. How was this king supposed to be selected?

Based on our lesson today, why was it so important that Yahweh make their selection?

God's first choice was never for any human authority to govern Israel. They weren't to be like other nations. But if, in her obstinacy, she chose to have an earthly king, then Yahweh was supposed to make the selection.

If He handpicked the nation's leader, then He would still remain the ultimate authority. The king would fall under His headship and could be held accountable to the prescribed divine requirements (Deut. 17:16-20). But if Israel did the choosing, over time God Himself would be lost under a pile of political red tape. Their new king would get the credit for their success as a nation and garner the position of authority that rightfully belonged to

Yahweh. Eventually, as seen in the case of King Saul's leadership, they would be led away from God.

Throughout this entire segment of the story Yahweh's voice is conspicuously omitted. In their eager desire for an authority figure, they neglected the One they already had. No matter how cohesive and wholehearted their proposal, their unwillingness to seek and wait for the direction of God was a step in the wrong direction.

They had gotten swept up in the fanfare of triumph, selecting their own leader outside of Yahweh's counsel. Their emotions didn't lead them well.

To you, O Lord, I lift up my soul. O my God, in You I trust.
Psalm 25:1-2

TOO FAST, TOO SOON

I pray you've been encouraged by how our weaknesses, when submitted to God, can be parlayed into demonstrations of His strength. But be careful: our excitement and zeal over what God does can lead us astray just as quickly as any pain or discomfort can.

Adversity and prosperity—two different stations in life. And yet both can trigger the same inappropriate responses, decisions, and dependence. So when God miraculously provides for us, we must guard against our tendency to give credit and loyalty to another.

Here are some suggestions to help. Read the following principles and the accompanying passages. Then record how they speak to you.

1. Pinpoint your tendencies. Ask the Lord to clearly show you where you normally turn for comfort, acceptance, approbation, and connection during good (and bad) times in your life.

"Put me on trial, Lord, and cross-examine me. Test my motives and my heart" (Ps. 26:2, NLT).

_____

_____

_____

2. Restructure your allegiances. Recommit to a God-centered existence in which you consistently acknowledge and seek God before turning to other things or people for approval or acceptance.

"Seek the Kingdom of God above all else, and He will give you everything you need" (Luke 12:31, NLT).

_____

_____

_____

3. Rearrange your priorities. Refuse to indulge improper passions. Restructure your life to exclude the idols that have become your go-to activities or relationships. Cement boundaries in place and enlist accountability to keep you on track.

"Therefore if you have been raised up with Christ, keep seeking the things above, where Christ is, seated at the right hand of God. Set your mind on the things above, not on the things that are on earth" (Col. 3:1-2).

_____

_____

_____

What would the practical implementation of these three principles look like in your life this week?

Today my #LessonsFromGideon are:

THE PROBLEM WITH ME

I think we know each other well enough now for me to just be honest with you about something. Don't judge me, OK?

At more times in my life than I'd like to admit, I left an idol or two tucked away in my heart well after God's Spirit had shown me they were there. Instead of dealing with them, I just kept quiet and marched along as if everything was in order, doing my best to ignore and outrun the conviction. I knew that opening myself up to their removal would require an uncomfortable transformation I didn't want to deal with right then. So I just didn't.

Dealing with yourself takes courage, my friend—a boldness that eludes some folks all the way to the grave. So let me just tell you that I'm proud of you. Together we've walked steadily and courageously down Israel's side of the track. We haven't tiptoed gingerly along in hopes of hopping off before the Holy Spirit realized we were there. We've marched flatfooted for three full days this week. The fact that you've still opened up your workbook today means you aren't messin' around.

So, bravo, my friend! Bravo! Today and tomorrow, we're still headed in the same direction, but we're going to do it on Gideon's side of the track. If you'll jump over here with me, you'll see that his vantage point will lend itself to a more subtle, internal perspective.

Israel's problem was making an idol out of someone else. Gideon's problem was making one out of himself.

CREDIT APPROVAL

Ever find that crisp, white envelope from a credit card company in your mailbox— so shiny and flashy among the other scraps of junk mail? Your name is inscribed across the front with the words "You've Been Pre-Approved" emblazoned below.

They're offering you a line of credit you never thought you could claim— offering status and prominence. You're sold on the idea before you even get back to your front door. The glimmer of the big print blinds you to the small—the details you don't care to notice today. So you accept the credit. Plus the staggering interest that's tagged onto it.

Look at the passage in the margin. To what does Gideon clearly say no?

What part of their statement does he not address?

Since Gideon has been quite outspoken throughout this entire chapter, what does this omission imply?

> Then the men of Israel said to Gideon, "Rule over us, both you and your son, also your son's son, for you have delivered us from the hand of Midian." But Gideon said to them, "I will not rule over you, nor shall my son rule over you; the LORD shall rule over you."
> Judges 8:22-23

Sometimes we shout a more blatant message by what we don't say than by what we do. Actions may speak louder than words, but inaction speaks too. Like when I asked my husband for his approval on an outfit I'd carefully put together, and he gave me a blank stare before turning on his heel and marching out the door. There I was, left alone in the robotic model-pose I'd been striking. His feelings about my choice of clothing were clear even though he hadn't said a word. In fact, they were clear *because* he hadn't said a word.

Israel gave God's glory to Gideon—"for you have delivered us from the hand of Midian" (v. 22). Blinded by the recognition, Gideon ignored the small print on the contract of their affection. By not saying a word, he signed on the dotted line, accepting credit he hadn't earned nor could he ultimately afford. It was a choice that, in the end, would cost everyone dearly.

How do you tend to deal with admiration from others?
- ☐ accept it
- ☐ deflect it
- ☐ try to escape it
- ☐ other _____

What, if any, are the positives and negatives of this response?

The appreciation of others will most certainly come your way as God demonstrates His strength in your weakness. His work almost always garners this kind of response. So I want you to hear me clearly: nothing is wrong when people celebrate and honor the work God has done through you, or when you honor it in others. It's what you do with the admiration that's important. Where it settles in your heart and mind is what's critical.

Just averting a compliment is not always the best reaction. A sincere acceptance of someone's accolade is actually more gracious than the false humility of an artificial deflection.

Both extremes must be tempered with an authentic gratitude, as well as something that Gideon omitted: a deliberate and purposeful redirection of the admirer's attention to the One who truly deserves the acclaim. When we neglect to boldly credit God as the Source behind our success, we begin, even if inadvertently, to assume the throne that should be His. Let me tell you, that throne comes with a high price tag of responsibility that only God Himself has the resources to cover.

> **Prayerfully write Psalm 115:1 in the margin.**
>
> **List some practical ways you can authentically live out this verse.**

A conversation on idolatry normally compels us to look at the external people or things that might be misplaced in our lives. Gideon's side of the track invites a more understated, introspective approach. Could it be that we might be our own idol? The following are four indicators of self-idolatry.

1. Do I defer credit and recognition to God, or do I reserve it, even secretly, for myself?
2. Do I place more value on my own logic than God's Word?
3. Am I more passionate about pursuing my own comforts than God's mission for my life?
4. Am I tempted to make Christianity convenient by making up my own rules and parameters for relating to God rather than connecting to Him on His terms?

> **Review these four indicators slowly and thoughtfully. Mark the portions that stand out to you. Which resonates most with you personally and why?**

LOUD AND CLEAR

Gideon's refusal to become king has been noted as one of the most noble incidents in all of Scripture. Few would have rejected the offer of such an esteemed position with all of its personal perks and generational provision. Yet his actions tell a completely different story. Hidden behind his verbal rejection is a secret agenda that reeks of a swollen ego and a full dose of self-gratification.

> **Consider each of the following verses from Judges 8 and complete each sentence.**
>
> **8:21—Gideon took …**
>
> **8:24—Gideon requested …**
>
> **8:27—Gideon created …**
>
> **8:30—Gideon had …**
>
> **8:30—Gideon also had …**
>
> **8:31—Gideon named his son …**

Each of these actions pointed to the heart of a man who had become his own potentate. He didn't take just any ornaments. Seduced and lured by the symbolism of influence and power, he took only the ones worn by kings. He didn't say he was king, but he would own the jewelry that classified him as one.

When he requested a portion of the spoils of war from his kinsmen, he assumed a position of national authority. Their gifts were a symbolic gesture of their submission. Then he used the lavish offering to build an image that was an affront to the parameters for worship set by Yahweh. It became a snare for the entire nation.

Gideon's family life was incriminating as well. His harem and brood of children could only be sustained by the riches that would normally accompany a king's position. The mere fact that he had 70 sons (not to mention daughters) is a clear indication that he was sitting pretty. Finally, if anyone still doubted that Gideon was at the top of the Israelite chain of command, he put all doubt to rest by naming his son Abimelech—"my Father, a king." See the *melek* in there?

The offering given to Gideon amounted to a royal treasure: 1,700 shekels (or 43 pounds) was a colossal gift and didn't even include the other royal adornments and garments removed from Midian's kings.

Circle any actions from the previous paragraphs that fit into one of the four indicators of self-idolatry on page 166. Explain the connection between them.

Gideon verbally rejected the title, but lived in a way that revealed he had assumed the position. It's easy to say the Lord is our King, but our actions will tell the real story. Are we submitted to His authority? Honoring His guidelines? Crediting Him with our successes?

Spend the next twenty-four hours watching yourself closely, asking the Holy Spirit to convict you of hidden sin. What are your tendencies? Do you defer to your own truth or to God's? Do your actions reflect His heart or your flesh's desire? Are you more concerned with your comfort or His glory? Come back here often to record anything the Lord reveals to you.

Today my #LessonsFromGideon are:

DAY 5
CONVENIENT CHRISTIANITY

"Come get your shoes out of the living room, buddy." I looked into the eyes of my eight-year-old with an intensity that let him know I meant business. His habit of leaving his shoes all over the house was wearing on me. He needed to put them back where they belonged instead of wherever they landed when he was through with them.

He looked a bit bewildered as I leaned into his personal space. "Mom," he said, "I like leaving them here so I can just grab 'em when I go outside to play." My expression showed that I had no intention of repeating my instructions. He picked up his shoes and headed to his room. As he passed me, I delayed him just long enough to remind him that his convenience was not more important than his obedience. His ease didn't trump my rules.

This is the stark reality about to hit us in our final lesson—the tension that sometimes exists between our convenience and God's regulations.

> **Read Judges 8:27 in the margin. Mark what Gideon made and where he put it. Below, record how it affected Israel.**

> Gideon made it into an ephod, and placed it in his city, Ophrah, and all Israel played the harlot with it there, so that it became a snare to Gideon and his household.
> Judges 8:27

Fueled by the lure of convenience, Gideon sacrificed commitment to God's order. His colossal error would have horrific, long-lasting repercussions.

GOD ON MY TERMS

The high priest's ephod was a <u>mysterious garment</u>, an apron of sorts, possessing many prominent features that contained beautiful symbolism. For example, it held twelve precious stones that covered the breastplate in four rows of three, representing the twelve tribes of Israel (Ex. 28: 17-21). Most notable of all the meticulous details were the Urim and the Thummin, two flat stones secured within the front of the vest. When exposed, they would somehow relay Yahweh's guidance and instruction to the high priests and ultimately to His people.

> Wouldn't it be intriguing to know how the ephod relayed God's instruction? No one really knows for sure but one theory offers that an inexplicable light flashed from one stone to indicate affirmation and from the other to signify a negative response.

Theologian Jeff Lucas argues that Urim means "to curse" and Thummim means "to be perfect." Thus when both stones displayed the Urim, the answer was negative. When both displayed the Thummin, the answer was affirmative. When one of each was forward-facing, the response was "no reply."[1]

What was the main purpose for the high priest's ephod?

The term ephod sometimes referred not only to the costly garment itself but also (in pagan environments) to any image or idol over which it might be draped. This is probably true in Gideon's case, seeing the large amount of gold involved (8:26). We aren't given details of the image, but no matter what it was, the purpose of the ephod was still the same—to hear directly from Yahweh.

Shiloh had been authorized by Yahweh as the religious center for the people (see Week 5, Day 3). Turn to the Geography of Gideon map and draw a line between this location and Ophrah and write "35 miles."

According to Exodus 28:4, who were the only people sanctioned to wear the holy garment?

How would these two factors have caused difficulty?

Talk about inconvenient! A 35-mile trip would have required at least two days of travel by foot. And having no priestly position, Gideon could not have entered the holy place once he got there.

After his personal encounters with God in the winepress and with the fleece, as well as the divine demonstration of success against the Midianites, Gideon may have felt like an exception—as if divine order no longer applied to him. He thought he could relate to God on his own terms. He thought he could make up new rules and expect Yahweh to acquiesce to them.

In a sense, Gideon had become addicted to hearing from God—so much so, that he prioritized hearing God over God Himself. So, he created his own ephod—easier to get to, more convenient to commune with, closer to home.

Flip back to yesterday's lesson. Which of the four indicators of self-idolatry fits Gideon's action?

Now, before we go pointing our finger at ol' Gideon, consider your own relationship with God in light of his example. How do you respond when God's plan requires more effort or energy than you'd hoped to expend?

- When receiving God's guidance requires long-term patience?
- When honoring God with your wealth becomes particularly sacrificial?
- When reading and understanding the Bible requires more time than simply scanning a supplemental resource?
- When gathering with the local church means forging through a rainstorm you'd rather avoid?
- When living in accordance with His moral standard means sticking out like a sore thumb among your peers?

What are some ways you've noticed Christians seeking to make Christianity fit their terms?

We are often inclined to shuffle our spiritual feet and do a little hypocritical jig around God's standards when the stakes are higher than we'd planned, just as cleverly as Gideon did. The more securely we become seated on the throne of our own lives, the more temptation to tweak God's plan to accommodate our comforts.

How have you been tempted to make your relationship with God easier or more convenient?

As we near the close of Gideon's story and our study, ask yourself, *Will I commit to God's order even when it jeopardizes my convenience?* Because the truth is that commitment is not always in stride with convenience. So, we have to make a conscious decision to choose holy allegiance with full knowledge that our ease will not always be placated.

Commitment trumps convenience.
#LessonsFromGideon

THE GOOD INTENTION

We've spent ample time considering the negative aspects of Gideon's action but, let's at least give him this much: his choice may have started with good intentions.

Put yourself in Gideon's sandals for a moment. What might have been his intentions when constructing the ephod in Ophrah?

Read Judges 8:33 in the margin. What does this verse suggest about what Gideon did before his death?

> Then it came about, as soon as Gideon was dead, that the sons of Israel again played the harlot with the Baals, and made Baal-berith their god.
> Judges 8:33

Strong leadership was conspicuously missing during the era of the judges. The high priest was apparently not functioning actively among the people. So Gideon's desire to step into a leadership role and offer the people a place to turn for spiritual governance is understandable. Perhaps even noble. Additionally, with Shiloh so far removed from the path of their everyday lives, he may have rightfully intended to refocus the people's attention back on God by bringing the ephod near.

For forty years (v. 28), with the ephod stationed illegitimately in Ophrah, Israel lived in relative peace. But the deceiving blanket of solace that fell across the land disguised the devastating idolatry spreading through their culture. For all those decades, it had been wearing away Israel's spiritual fiber.

Gideon made the ephod into nothing more than the proverbial rabbit's foot—a superstitious image disconnected from the one true God. After his death, the people, no longer restrained by Gideon's presence, slipped further down an idolatrous slope, spurred on by the image their leader had created. His good intentions weren't enough to neutralize the consequences of his disobedience and disrespect for God's divine order.

Open your Bible to read the final two verses of our study, Judges 8:34-35. Make a list of the effects of Gideon's ephod after his death.

What are some of the modern consequences you've seen of convenient Christianity?

Good intentions are not enough—not enough to honor God, not enough to sustain your spiritual growth, not enough to keep your spiritual legacy intact for generations to come. You and I cannot walk away from this study just intending to walk in accordance with what we've learned; we have to start doing it—one spiritual foot in front of the other, in obedience to God. Right now. Today.

I'm telling you, God is going to demonstrate His strength through you. He is. He wouldn't have kept you in these pages, learning these lessons if He weren't preparing you for something spectacular. And, praise His glorious name, neither your story nor mine needs to end like Gideon's, no matter what stage of the journey we are on. We can choose to convert our good intentions into obedient actions.

Keep Him first until the end of your days.

Pursue Him above His benefits with all your might.

Prioritize His way and His Word until you hear Him say, "Well done."

Expect your weakness to be a platform for His strength.

Carry on in confidence, my friend.

The Lord is with you, Mighty Warrior.

Until we meet again.

ENDNOTES

Week One
1. John Marshall Lang, *Gideon and the Judges: A Study* (New York: Revell, 1834), 87.

Week Two
1. Logos Bible Software ed. 5, Bellingham, WA. "Gideon" from *The Anchor Yale Bible Dictionary*.
2. Logos Bible Software ed. 5, Bellingham, WA. "Jether" from *Enhance Brown-Driver-Briggs Hebrew and English Lexicon*.
3. Jeff Lucas, *Gideon: Power from Weakness* (Franklin, TN: Authentic Publishers, 2004), 91

Week Three
1. Stephen M. Miller, *Who's Who and Where's Where in the Bible* (Uhrichsville, OH: Barbour Publishing, 2004), 126.
2. Logos Bible Software ed. 5, Bellingham, WA. "Gideon Summons the Israelites" from *Enhance Brown-Driver-Briggs Hebrew and English Lexicon*.

Week Four
1. Lang, *Gideon and the Judges*, 102.
2. Richard Booker, *The Miracle of the Scarlet Thread* (Shippensburg, PA: Destiny Image Publishers, 2008), 129.
3. Lang, *Gideon and the Judges*, 104.
4. Lang, *Gideon and the Judges*, 101.
5. Lang, *Gideon and the Judges*, 118.
6. James B. Jordan, *Judges: God's War against Humanism* (Tyler, TX: Geneva Ministries, 1985), 130.
7. Lang, *Gideon and the Judges*, 136

Week Five
1. Logos Bible Software ed. 5, Bellingham, WA. from *The New American Commentary*.

Week Six
1. Lucas, *Gideon: Power from Weakness*, 171.

Session 7
VIEWER GUIDE

NOTES

JUST YOU AND ME

LEADER GUIDE

Thank you for joining me on the journey through the story of Gideon, and may I give you a double portion of thanks for leading a group in the study? Gideon has long been both a great hero of the faith and an example of how tragically we can fail in our faith walk. I pray that God will greatly bless you as you study His Word and that Gideon will come off the page for you. I pray that his positive example will inspire your group and his negative example will warn us all.

If one thing unites us as believers, it most certainly is our weakness. In this Christian life, all who are honest come to echo the words of Paul the apostle: "For I know that nothing good lives in me, that is, in my flesh. For the desire to do what is good is with me, but there is no ability to do it" (Rom. 7:18). Gideon's story displays and addresses our weakness in a startling manner.

Through the study I hope you and your group will grasp the reality that God intends to use our weaknesses as the key to unlocking His strength. When we follow our natural tendency to hide our weakness, we reap a host of negative results (Prov. 28:13, James 4:6). When we cease hiding our weaknesses, our God uses them to demonstrate His incalculable strength.

Gideon: Your Weakness, God's Strength is designed to be a video-driven Bible study. Each week you'll show a video teaching. You'll find detailed information on how to access the videos on the card inserted in the back of the Bible study book. If your group doesn't have adequate Internet connection for video streaming, DVD sets are available for purchase at lifeway.com/gideon. That is where you will also find promotional tools and other helpful resources.

We suggest 90 minutes for weekly meetings for time to view the video session and discuss, but you may tailor the group time to fit members' needs. Each of the following session guides contains more questions than you'll have time to discuss. Prayerfully choose those you will use to stimulate discussion in your group. You may print those discussion questions you select. You may even consider the option of distributing the questions to your group.

Every group is different. Your women may be best served by discussing several of the questions each week, or they may have very productive meetings by simply sharing their hashtag statements. Your purpose is to encourage them to engage in the study and to guide them to process what they learn. If they apply the lessons of Gideon to their lives, you will have been a good and faithful group leader.

Set up a comfortable environment for your discussion time. You may choose to serve snacks and drinks each week. Arrange seating in a circle so all women can see each other. Much of your group time will be spent conversing about your own stories. Make sure women know that confidentiality is expected to make meetings a safe place to share their stories.

Start promptly to honor everyone's time. If your group is larger than 8 to 10 women, watch the videos together and then split into small groups for discussion. Take note of the video times, as they vary each week. Explain to your participants that you will facilitate the discussion, but you will not be lecturing. You will be learning together. Pray for the women during your daily time with God. Pray that the members will hear God's Word and respond.

Before your first session, prepare a sign-up sheet with names, email addresses, and phone numbers. If possible, have someone make copies for everyone in the group during the session. Put the list, extra pens, pencils, Bibles, and member books out before each session.

STARTING A BIBLE STUDY

1. Enlist volunteers to facilitate discussion groups. Ask women to be in prayer that God will prepare the hearts of the participants and draw them to Him.

2. Build a network of ownership for the study by enlisting those who will enlist others and share the tasks below. The more women you involve in the planning, the greater the success your group will experience.

3. Secure a room or home and decide on a time for each week's study.

4. Determine if snacks will be served and who will bring them.

5. Organize childcare if needed.

6. Publicize the study in your church and community. Share about the study with your friends and neighbors; use the promotional video segment during church services or other events.

7. Supply member books for the participants to purchase at the introductory session. Make scholarships available for those who cannot pay.

8. Access your videos using the scratch-off code in the back of your book. Note the viewer guide answers appear online at *lifeway.com/gideon*, and on p. 189.

SESSION ONE

Before the Session

1. Preview the video for session 1.
2. Consider procuring chalk, masking tape, string, or some other material for the end of the session. If you are in a place where you can, mark a circle on the floor or in some other way symbolically enact the prayer Priscilla used to close the session.
3. Read the Introduction (p. 5) and About the Author (p. 4). Underline a few key phrases as a reminder for step 2 of During the Session.

During the Session

1. What memories do you have centered around Gideon? Have you studied him and his story? What do you associate with Gideon?
2. Discuss the theme of the study: our weaknesses, God's strength. Introduce the study using the phrases you underlined in the Introduction and About the Author.
3. Direct members to pages 6-7 for the session 1 viewer guide. Show session 1 [56:39].
4. If time permits, ask what stood out in the video. What did they learn about Gideon? How do they see Gideon's story impacting their own?
5. Explain that each week will consist of five days of homework. Encourage members to complete all the work.
6. Share prayer requests. Pray for your participants. Pray for their requests and that they will be challenged by studying Gideon.

SESSION TWO

Before the Session

1. Preview the video for session 2.
2. Complete week 1 daily study and note items to discuss in group.

During the Session

1. Welcome participants as they enter. Offer snacks or drinks, if available.
2. Don't force anyone to share, but gently remind participants this is a safe environment for sharing.

3. Ask what hashtag statements they jotted down during the week.
4. Direct members to pages 38-39 for the session 2 viewer guide. Show session 2 [40:26].
5. For group discussion, choose from the following questions:

Day 1: God's People in Paradise
- How many Bible chapters tell Gideon's story?
- In which book of the Bible are these chapters found?
- What orders had God given the Israelites for settling the land (p. 10)?
- What "iron chariots" of intimidation keep believers from moving forward in complete obedience to God today (p. 11)?
- How do you see the Deliverance Principle impacting your life (question p. 12 and Digging Deeper I)?
- What comforts or perceived sense of security would you have to abandon to fully obey God's instructions (p. 13)?

Day 2: You Again?
- Have you experienced a problem that was an extension of a difficulty someone didn't fully conquer in the past (p. 16)?
- How do you respond to the statement: today's difficulties are often a result of yesterday's disobedience (p. 18)?
- What, if any, significance do you attach to the fact that the number of Midianites left alive in Moses' day equals the number of soldiers in Gideon's original army (p. 19)?

Day 3: God's Story, My Story
- Describe the cycle of redemption in your own words (p. 22).
- What adjectives would you use to describe the state of the Israelites during the stages of decline and consequence (p. 24)?
- What does Judges 2:18 reveal about the heart of God for His people, even when they're suffering the consequences of their sin (p. 24)?
- What realm of your life do you think God wants you to concentrate on while doing this study (p. 26)?

Day 4: Empowered to Act
- Review the hand signs: "Judges were people who were ...
  1. called by God (hands making a megaphone)
  2. empowered by God (arms out, flexing bicep muscles)
  3. to unify the people of God (hands in front, with fingers interlaced, turned toward yourself)
  4. so they could stand against the enemy of God (fingers interlaced, turned out to face away from yourself)."
- What connections do you see between the judges' role in the Old Testament and the role of modern believers (p. 29)?

- How do you think the church fares today in being one body of believers (p. 30)?
- How can we remain true to biblical beliefs and still be unified in the body of Christ today? What do you think we must not do?
- What four attributes did you identify as necessary to maintain harmony among believers (p. 30)?

Day 5: Turning the Tide

- What were two primary reasons Israel was faltering (p. 34)?
- Which reason do you think has been the most central to moral decline in our day (p. 34)?
- How can you creatively share the truth of God with younger people (p. 35)?
- How can you deliberately position yourself to learn (p. 35)?
- What similarities did you identify between ancient Baalism and modern humanism (p. 36)?

3. Close by asking for prayer requests and praying for group members. Encourage group members to meet with God daily through their study this week.

SESSION THREE

Before the Session

1. Preview the video for session 3.
2. Complete week 2 daily study and note items to discuss in group.

During the Session

1. Welcome participants as they enter. Offer snacks or drinks, if available.
2. Ask what hashtag statements they jotted down during the week.
3. Direct members to pages 66-67 for the session 3 viewer guide. Play the session video [39:23].
4. For group discussion, choose from the following questions:

Day 1: Commissioning Gideon

- What summary idea do you take from Ephesians 1:18-19?
- What expectations do you think believers have of how God reveals Himself?
- How have these expectations been formed?
- How might these beliefs keep people from recognizing a God encounter in their lives?

Day 2: Above Ground Observations

- God used Gideon's everyday task of threshing in his calling and life task. How do you see God possibly using one or more of your daily tasks in the calling He has for your life?
- What do your routine tasks say to you about God's faithfulness?

Day 3: Overlooking the Obvious
- What questions have you had for God during periods of difficulty?
- What insights did you find in the Scriptures you chose to look up on page 53 (from Mic. 6:8, 1 Thess. 4:3; 5:18, Eph. 6:6, Matt. 22:37-38)?
- Why do you think we so often fail to connect what we know God has done previously with facing our present situations (p. 53)?
- How do you see in Gideon's story hints of our tendency to stress our own logic over God's truth (p. 54)?

Day 4: Who Do You Think You Are?
- How would you explain the hashtag statement that behavior does not determine identity (p. 56)?
- Why do you think it is critical for believers to understand their identity before moving forward into their destiny (p. 57)?
- How have you seen an incorrect or malformed spiritual identity hamper someone's spiritual success (p. 57)?
- Which of the pairs of terms on page 57 best describe a disparity you've dealt with between your self-perception and a biblical perception of who you are in Christ. Why did you choose that pair?
- How do you most often deal with what God says about you (p. 58)?
- What would receiving, believing, and walking in what God says about you do in your life? What would change about the next twenty-four hours if you believed what God said (p. 58)?

Day 5: Gideon's Assignment
- Why do you think Gideon beginning his work by destroying the altar of Baal was critical to Israel's overarching success (p. 61)?
- In Genesis 18:19, what did God tell Abraham to concentrate on prior to experiencing the fulfillment of His promises (p. 62)?
- In what ways have you felt like Gideon when he tore down his family altar by night (p. 63)?

SESSION FOUR

Before the Session
1. Preview the video for session 4.
2. Complete week 3 daily study and note items to discuss in group. Pay special attention to group discussion questions.
3. Contact any members needing encouragement.

During the Session

1. Welcome participants as they enter. Offer snacks or drinks, if available.
2. Invite members to share hashtag statements from this week.
3. Direct members to pages 92-93 for the session 4 viewer guide. Play the session video [40:39].
4. For group discussion, choose from the following questions:

Day 1: The Key to Our Strength

- When you focus on your weaknesses, what effect does this have on your emotions, self-image, confidence, and ability to move forward (p. 70)?
- How do you usually deal with a situation when you feel outmatched (p. 72)?
- What would redirecting your focus away from your weaknesses look like in practical terms for you (p. 73)?
- What strategic things do you think believers can do to redirect their attention off themselves and onto the Lord (p. 73)?

Day 2: Less Is More

- On some occasions we have all credited ourselves, or others, with something God did. What do you think contributes to such over-sight (p. 74)?
- In what ways have you seen misdirected credit lead to misplaced trust or unhealthy desires and choices in your life or the life of someone else (p. 75)?
- Discuss the statement in the margin of page 76: "Humility is not thinking unkindly about oneself. It's being willing to set oneself aside for a more important purpose." Ask: How might we err on the side of pride when we feel overly competent or the side of self-focus when we feel incompetent?
- Invite members to share from page 76 words that contribute to pride and words that stimulate humility in their lives? What lessons can we draw from the exercise?
- What practical strategies can you put in place to foster humility (p. 76)?

Day 3: Double Trouble

- Has your confidence in your ability and in God been enhanced as you've moved forward with less? How (p. 79)?
- Has the Lord been stripping anything from your life that may have been dampening your spiritual sensitivity, distracting you from God's purposes, or heightening your fleshly desires and tendencies (p. 81)?

Day 4: Letting Go
- How do you see the "bigger is better" mentality emphasized in your spheres of influence? How has this pressure affected you? Your family (p. 82)?
- If you had to pinpoint an area of your life to label "the 300"—an area where you feel depleted or deficient—what category(s) would it fall into (p. 83)?
- How do any of the thoughts on page 84 relate to your experience and difficulty in letting go?

Day 5: The Unseen Supply
- What conclusions do you draw from the similarities and differences between the armor of God passage in Ephesians 6:10-17 and Gideon's situation (p. 89)?
- If you had to pinpoint something that most often distracts you from remembering and using your unseen supply, what would it be (p. 91)?

SESSION FIVE

Before the Session
1. Preview the video for session 5.
2. Complete week 4 daily study and note items to discuss in group. Pay special attention to group discussion questions.
3. Contact any members needing encouragement.

During the Session
1. Welcome participants as they enter. Offer snacks or drinks.
2. Invite members to share hashtag statements they have written or seen from others this week.
3. Direct members to pages 118-119 for the session 5 viewer guide. Play the session video [44:33].
4. For group discussion, choose from the following questions:

Day 1: The God of Patience
- So far, what circumstances can you recall from the story of Gideon that reveal God's patience (p. 95)?
- While you've been in this study, how have you seen the long-suffering of God demonstrated to you (p. 96)?
- Based on the fact that God initiated the conversation that sent Gideon to eavesdrop on the Midianite camp, what can you infer about how God felt about Gideon's need for reassurance (p. 97)?

Day 2: Gideon's Gifts

- Which is more difficult for you: offering your gifts back to the Lord, offering your desires to the Lord, trusting Him with when your gifts are used, or trusting Him with how your gifts are used (p. 100)?
- What do you sense God asking you to do in this season of your life as you go through this study? What gifts has He given you to accomplish this task (p. 101)?
- What practical things could you do to "prepare" the gifts that the Lord has given you (p. 102)?
- Which part of this process is hardest for you: having the patience to faithfully prepare your gift or having the courage to present your gift to God (p. 102)?

Day 3: The Fleece, The Dew, and the Threshing Floor

- Are you easily satisfied with the confirmation God gives you or do you always need more (p. 106)?
- Why do you think God became angry with Moses in Exodus 4:1-14 but did not express anger to Gideon (p. 107)?
- What are the differences between seeking confirmation from God out of caution and seeking it because of doubt and disbelief (p. 107)?

Day 4: The "Dew" and the "Do" of Heaven

- How should the grace and favor bestowed on believers refresh us and make us different than the culture around us (p. 110)?
- What are three distinct ways you are different from the world around you (p. 110)?
- Are there any areas of your life that you no longer talk to God about because you feel like "that's just the way things are"? If so, what areas are they (p. 112)?

Day 5: Faith Squared

- How might the instruction to go listen to the talk in the Midianite camp underscore the patience and kindness of God even more than the other encouragements He granted Gideon (p. 114)?
- How can our group strategize to walk together in accountability long after this study is over, to remind each another of what God has accomplished (p. 115)?

SESSION SIX

Before the Session

1. Preview the video for session 6.
2. Complete week 5 daily study and note items to discuss in group. Pay special attention to group discussion questions.
3. Contact any members needing encouragement.

During the Session
1. Welcome participants as they enter.
2. Invite members to share hashtag statements they have written or seen from others this week.
3. Direct members to pages 146-147 for the session 6 viewer guide. Play the session video [44:52].
4. For group discussion, choose from the following questions:

Day 1: Unusual Weapons
- From the exercise on page 123, ask if anyone would be willing to share a difficult scenario facing her right now, her natural response, and a Holy Spirit–revealed divine weapon God has led her to use.
- What "logic" does the enemy typically use against you to disguise the spiritual nature of your struggles and to mask his role in the middle of them (p. 124)?
- How can some of the weaknesses in your life be a weapon for your warfare through which the power of Christ is most clearly seen (p. 125)?

Day 2: Finishing Well
- Might you ever be inclined to pacify your insecurity instead of staying inside the boundaries set up by God? If so, why do you feel the need to do this (p. 128)?

Day 3: Friendly Fire
- Recall the last time you were on the receiving end of a dose of criticism. What effect did it have on you (p. 131)?
- What tempts you to make critical comments or causes you to sometimes find it difficult to affirm another person (p. 131)?
- How have you seen feeling special and exceptional play into a critical nature (p. 133)?

Day 4: Weary, Yet Pursuing
- How have you responded to people or things that have not given you what you hoped they would? How was your response similar or dissimilar to Gideon's response (p. 139)?
- What does waiting on the Lord look like practically in your life (p. 139)?

Day 5: The Domino Effect
- Have any of your divine assignments taken a turn toward personal interests? If so, what circumstances have caused you to change your focus (p. 142)?
- How do you think our confidence and success become the enemy of our fellowship with God (p. 144)?
- How is your relationship with God affected when you feel weak and uncertain about yourself or a task? How is it affected when you are confident and secure (p. 145)?

SESSION SEVEN

Before the Session

1. Preview the video for session 7.
2. Complete week 6 daily study and note items to discuss in group. Pay special attention to group discussion questions.
3. Contact any members needing encouragement.

During the Session

1. Welcome participants as they enter.
2. Invite members to share hashtag statements they have written or seen from others this week.
3. Play the session video [27:15].
4. For group discussion, choose from the following questions:

Day 1: No Other Gods

- What insights did you gather from the interview questions on page 150?
- How did you define the word "idol" (p. 150)?
- Discuss this statement from the video message: "We are not human beings having a spiritual experience; we are spiritual beings having a human experience." How does this relate to your definition of an idol (p. 152)?

Day 2: Good to Bad, Bad to Worse

- Review the case studies on page 155-156. In what way would you say these things have become "rulers" in these women's lives?
- Have the two good things you chose from your interview begun to assume an illegitimate role of authority in your life? If so, how (p. 157)?
- What does the progression in Israel from calf worship to full-grown cow worship suggest to you about the potential of idolatry in our own lives (p. 158)?

Day 3: Feeling Fine

- In what ways can achievement, prosperity, and success contribute to a misdirection of loyalty (p. 160)?
- How does impatience play a role in idolatry for modern-day believers (p. 160)?
- Why was it so important that Yahweh select the king for the people of Israel (p. 161)?

Day 4: The Problem with Me

- What positives and negatives of your response to admiration did you identify (p. 165)?

- What are some practical ways you can authentically live out Psalm 115:1 (p. 166)?
- From the four questions/indicators of self-idolatry on page 166, which resonates most with you and why?

Day 5: Convenient Christianity
- In what ways do we seek to make Christianity fit our terms (p. 172)?
- What might have been Gideon's intentions when constructing the ephod in Ophrah (p. 172)?
- What were the results of Gideon's ephod (p. 173)?
- What are some of the modern consequences you've seen of convenient Christianity (p. 173)?

VIEWER GUIDE ANSWERS
Session 1:
moving forward; context; what was evil; again; own eyes; judges; called, empowered, unite, stand against; devastation, oppression 1. information, heads; teaching; young, listen. 2. hearts, passion. 3. doing, right.

Session 2:
unexpected; head, water, resurfaces; 1. powerful, reach. 2. position, calling; heart, circumstances; Scripture, true. 3. dictate, capability. came, appeared, looked.

Session 3:
Baal fighter; same person; record, work; tremble, fear; environment, posture; beginning, finish, end; stand, vantage point; too many. 1. same person. 2. going. 3. need, need.

Session 4:
patient, long-suffering; held, mercy. 1. saved. 2. changes. 3. positioned. worthy, worthy. 4. strengthened.

Session 5:
1. your, knees. 2. stance, victory. 3. assigned place. 4. right time. 5. right weapons.

Session 6:
1. authority? 2. credit? 3. deflect? 4. belongs? snare.

Also available
— from —
PRISCILLA
SHIRER

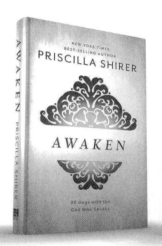

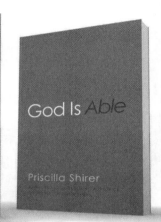

— For Kids —

Available where books are sold.

Other Studies by Priscilla

ELIJAH
7 sessions

Journey through the life and times of the prophet Elijah to discover how the fire on Mount Carmel was forged in the valley of famine. And how the emboldened, fiery faith you desire is being fashioned by God in your life right now.

lifeway.com/elijah

DISCERNING THE VOICE OF GOD
Revised & Expanded
7 sessions

Discover the root to clear and daily communication with God—humble obedience.

lifeway.com/discerningthevoiceofgod

THE ARMOR OF GOD
7 sessions

The enemy always fails miserably when he meets a woman dressed for the occasion. Develop your own personalized strategy to secure victory against the enemy.

lifeway.com/armorofgod

BREATHE
5 sessions

If you are weary, worn out, and exhausted, the concept of Sabbath will change your life. Challenge yourself to break your devotion to busyness and gain back your peace from Him alone.

lifeway.com/breathe

JONAH
7 sessions

Redefine interruption as God's invitation to do something greater than you could ever imagine. When Jonah was willing to allow God to interrupt his life, the result was city-wide revival.

lifeway.com/lifeinterrupted

ONE IN A MILLION
7 sessions

Only two out of two million Israelites crossed over into the Promised Land. Discover direction for your spiritual life and expect to see God move in miraculous ways.

lifeway.com/oneinamillion

Lifeway women

lifeway.com/priscillashirer
800.458.2772

Pricing and availability subject to change without notice.

ISRAELITE SETTLEMENT AND
THE LAND YET TO BE CONQUERED

▲ MOUNTAIN PEAK
LAND INHABITED BY ISRAELITES
AREAS YET TO BE CONQUERED
THE GEOGRAPHY OF GIDEON

AMURRU

36 E

Zedad

Byblos

Lebo-hamath

PHOENICIA

Valley of Lebanon

Sidon

Mt. Hermon

Damascus
Abana River

ARAM

Ahlab
Tyre
Litani River

Laish
(Dan)

MAACAH

Pharpar River

Beth-anath

Kitron

Kedesh

Lake
Huleh

Rehob
Achzib

Beth-shemesh

Hazor
Merom

GALILEE

GESHUR

Bashan

Acco

Aphek

Sea of
Galilee

Golan

Ashtaroth

Nahalal

Mt. Carmel ▲
Kishon River

Shimron
Mt. Tabor

Yarmuk River

MEDITERRANEAN
SEA

Yokneam

Jezreel Valley

Endor

Ophrah

Dor

Megiddo

Beth-shan

Ramoth-gilead

Taanach

GILEAD

Ibleam

Jabesh-gilead

Socoh

Jordan River

Mt. Ebal ▲

Succoth

Mahanaim

Mt. Gerizim ▲

Shechem

Jabbok River

AMMON

Aphek
Yarkon River

Tappuah

Penuel

Joppa

Shiloh

Jazer

Jogbehah

HILL COUNTRY
OF EPHRAIM

Shaalbim

Gibeon

Jericho

Heshbon

Rabbah
(Amman)

Gezer

Aijalon

Ashdod

Ekron

Beth-
shemesh

Jerusalem
(Jebus)

Mt. Nebo ▲

Bezer

Ashkelon

Gath

Bethlehem

Medeba

Eastern
Desert

Lachish

Amorites pressure tribe
of Dan near Aijalon
(Judg. 1:34–36)

Dibon

Gaza

Hebron

Aroer

Gerar

Ziklag

KENIZZITES

DEAD
SEA

Arnon River

JUDAH

KENITES
Arad

En-gedi

MOAB

Kir-hareseth

Beersheba

AMALEKITES

192

W. el-Arish

Tamar

EDOM

Zered River

Wilderness of Zin

Bozrah

0   10   20   30   40   50 Miles

0 10 20 30 40   50 Kilometers

34 E

35 E

36 E